# CONTENTS

"ATTACK! ATTACK! ATTACK!" ....................4

WAR WITH FRANCE ....................6

ENTER THE USA ....................12

THE US MILITARY GOES IN ....................20

ONGOING WAR ....................26

LIVING THROUGH THE WAR ....................36

THE ANTI-WAR MOVEMENT ....................44

VIETNAM UNITED ....................52

THE AFTERMATH OF CONFLICT ....................58

WHAT HAVE WE LEARNED? ....................66

TIMELINE ....................68

GLOSSARY ....................70

NOTES ON SOURCES ....................73

BIBLIOGRAPHY ....................76

FIND OUT MORE ....................77

INDEX ....................79

Words printed in **bold** are explained in the Glossary.

# "ATTACK! ATTACK! ATTACK!"

It was 31 January 1968, the first night of the Tet **Offensive** attacks on South Vietnam. The North Vietnamese planned to attack the South and their US **allies** on Tet, the Vietnamese New Year holiday, when no one would expect military action. Tuan Van Ban anxiously awaited his first combat mission. His **battalion** of the People's Army of Vietnam (PAVN) was to assault a US **Marine** base. Around midnight the battalion, camouflaged in dirt, moved in close to the perimeter fence of the base. They waited for dawn, too excited to rest. At 5.00 a.m. they fired a flare and detonated dynamite to blast holes in the fence. Mortar men and machine gunners fired into the base, bugles and whistles sounded, and the troops advanced, screaming "Attack! Attack! Attack!"

△ South Vietnamese General Nguyen Ngoc executes North Vietnamese soldier Nguyen Van Lém during the Tet Offensive. This shocking image, depicting the brutality of war, has become famous worldwide.

By the time the Americans retaliated with **artillery** fire, Tuan Van Ban and most of his battalion had penetrated the perimeter and raced to the communications centre. It was dark and chaotic, and bullets were flying everywhere. They destroyed as much equipment as possible and then withdrew. Around 20 had died in the attack, and 70 were wounded.[1]

## UNDER FIRE

Bob Gabriel was a US **GI** sent with his battalion to relieve the besieged town of Hue in South Vietnam. The fighting was ferocious. Under attack from the North Vietnamese, a helicopter dived in close, and his colonel yelled "Charge that machine gun." Bob's comrades made a run for it, leaving him alone with the machine gun. The Vietnamese stormed towards him, shooting continuously. He fired and ran, fired and ran. Somehow, he survived without a scratch. Finally, another group of soldiers came to escort him back to safety. They congratulated him for exposing himself to fire to save his comrades.[2]

### Bombs rain down

Dang Thuy Tram, a doctor in South Vietnam in 1969, gives a vivid description of what it was like to experience the Vietnam War as a **civilian**:

"An OV-10 [light US] plane circles several times above the hamlets, then launches a rocket down to Hamlet 13 … Immediately, two jets take turn[s] diving down. Where each bomb strikes, fire and smoke flare up; the **napalm** bomb flashes, then explodes in a red ball of fire, leaving dark, thick smoke that climbs into the sky. Still, the airplanes scream overhead, a series of bombs raining down with each pass, the explosions deafening … I sit with silent fury in my heart. Who is burned in that fire and smoke?"[3]

These episodes give us a glimpse of the 30-year Vietnam War, which involved the entire Vietnamese population, the armies of France and the United States, and troops from Australia, New Zealand, and South Korea. Why was a powerful nation like the United States pitted against a small South-East Asian country and what was the impact on Vietnam, its neighbours, and on the United States itself?

# WAR WITH FRANCE

France **colonized** Vietnam in the 19th century, and ruled it for more than 50 years. In 1887 France created the Indo-Chinese Union, which also included Cambodia. Laos was added in 1893. The French brutally put down those who resisted their authority. At the end of World War II, the **communist** leader Ho Chi Minh declared independence in North Vietnam. Between 1945 and 1954, France tried to take back control of Vietnam, while the North Vietnamese fought to unify the nation as an independent state.

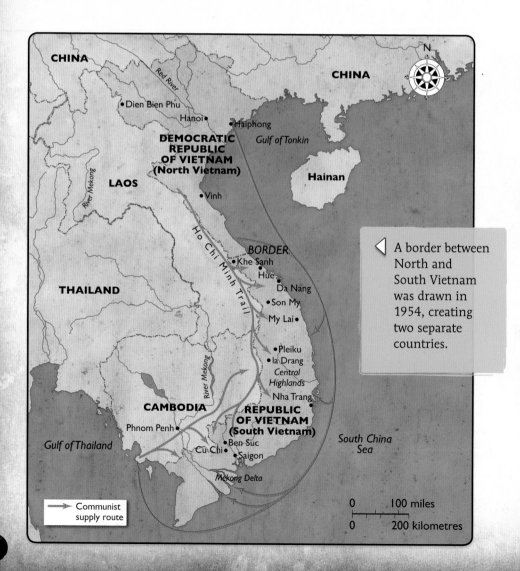

A border between North and South Vietnam was drawn in 1954, creating two separate countries.

## COLONIAL EXPLOITATION

The French originally took over Vietnam to **exploit** it economically. They established rubber plantations and mines, and paid low wages to their Vietnamese employees. The colonists seized much of the land from the Vietnamese peasants. By the late 1930s, about half the population was landless.[1] Also during colonial times, Chinese migrants settled in Vietnam and worked as traders, craftspeople, and labourers.

The Vietnamese resisted French rule from the start. In the 1920s, young radicals looked for ways to overthrow the French and introduce a new form of society. In 1930 Ho Chi Minh founded the Indo-Chinese Communist Party. Its aim was to free Vietnam from colonial rule.

## THE RISE OF THE VIET MINH

The Japanese army **occupied** Vietnam from 1940 and backed the French colonial government. As well as causing severe economic hardship, the occupation deepened the Vietnamese desire for independence. Vietnamese communists set up the Independence League of Vietnam (Viet Minh) in 1941 and worked to unify the population against the Japanese and the French. Although the Viet Minh was led by communists, it included many other kinds of **nationalists**, too.

In March 1945, Japan took over the government from France. At this time, there was a terrible famine in North Vietnam, which killed an estimated 2 million people.[2] The Viet Minh was the only organization to try to tackle the desperate situation and they saved perhaps 100,000 lives.[3] For this, the Viet Minh won the support of the people. In September 1945, Ho Chi Minh declared the independence of North Vietnam, also known as the Democratic Republic of Vietnam (the DRV), in its capital city Hanoi.

### Seize the rice!

During the 1945 famine in North Vietnam, the Japanese did nothing to transport rice from the Mekong Delta in the South. However, wealthy people, soldiers, and police in North Vietnam still had food. The Viet Minh advised people to attack the rice warehouses. Young men would overpower the guards and others would grab the rice and run away.[4]

You can find out more at: http://amchamvietnam.com/index.php?id=3121

## THE GREAT POWERS BACK FRANCE

Ho Chi Minh hoped that the United States would support an independent Vietnam. This was a reasonable assumption because in the early 1940s, the US government had supported the idea of colonized countries gaining freedom from foreign rule. However, Ho Chi Minh's hopes were soon dashed. The leaders of the world powers had already decided how to divide up the post-war world at the Potsdam Conference in July 1945. France was to be allowed to keep its **colonies** in Indo-China. It was agreed that Britain would restore order in South Vietnam and return the country to French control. The Chinese army would do the same in the North.

### The Geneva negotiations

At the peace talks after Dien Bien Phu (see page 9), Vietnam was divided at the 17th parallel into two separate countries. North Vietnam remained under Ho Chi Minh, while Bao Dai was to stay in power in South Vietnam. Nationwide elections were to achieve a final political settlement but, in 1955, Bao Dai's successor Ngo Dinh Diem refused to hold them.

The French army soon replaced the British in the South and began to reassert its power. In November 1946, the French began the fight to regain North Vietnam, too. They seized the northern city of Haiphong and in December, fighting broke out in Hanoi. During the late 1940s, it appeared that France might succeed in its aims. Then in 1949, a communist government took power in China. In January 1950, both the **Soviet Union** and China recognized North Vietnam. Both offered military equipment and support to the fledgling state.

## THE COLD WAR HEATS UP

The United States reacted quickly, announcing its recognition of French-backed South Vietnam under the former Vietnamese emperor Bao Dai, as did Britain. Vietnam took on strategic importance in the Cold War – the tensions between the United States and its Western allies, and the Soviet Union and other communist countries. In June 1950, the Cold War turned hot in South-East Asia when communist North Korea invaded South Korea, and the Korean War began.

To the United States, it seemed vital for France to hold the line against communism in Vietnam. By the end of 1950, the US government had allocated $100 million in economic and military aid to France and the South Vietnamese government.[5]

Despite US support for its enemies, from 1950 North Vietnam began to make advances in the war. The military supplies from its communist allies helped. More crucially, Ho Chi Minh won support from the people by introducing **land reform**, education, and healthcare in the areas under his control. Most Vietnamese people supported independence rather than French rule. Yet North Vietnam needed an impressive military victory to force France to negotiate.

## DIEN BIEN PHU

In 1954 Viet Minh fighters prepared their forces to attack the last major French stronghold at Dien Bien Phu. A quarter of a million civilians carried pieces of Chinese heavy artillery on their backs through the rainforest and over mountains to trenches surrounding the French forces. After reassembling their large guns, the Viet Minh bombarded the French positions. After an exhausting and bloody campaign that lasted around eight weeks, the Viet Minh finally won a resounding victory against the French, and the foreign power surrendered.

▽  Here you can see Vietnamese soldiers attacking the French military base at Dien Bien Phu in 1954.

# HO CHI MINH (1890–1969)

Ho Chi Minh was born in a village in central Vietnam. As a young man in 1911, he took a job as a cook on a French ship. After three years, he moved to Britain, then in 1917 to France, where he worked as a gardener, waiter, and sweeper, amongst other jobs.

Ho Chi Minh was inspired by the Russian **Revolution** of 1917. The communist Bolshevik Party had seized power and taken control of land and industries, promising to provide for everyone according to their need. Ho Chi Minh joined the French Communists in 1920. He went to Moscow, Russia, in late 1923, where he met the leaders of Soviet communism. During the 1920s and 1930s, he worked for communism in several countries, including China and Thailand.

▽ Ho Chi Minh, seen here at a rally in 1955, was a skilful diplomat. He acquired aid from China and the Soviet Union even though the two communist powers were often at odds with each other.

## UNITING THE PEOPLE

In 1941 Ho Chi Minh returned to Vietnam and established the Viet Minh. Rather than immediately working for a communist revolution, he wanted to unite the Vietnamese people in the nationalist goal of obtaining freedom from colonial rule. In 1945 he declared the independence of North Vietnam as a first step towards that goal. He used words based on the US Declaration of Independence: "All men are born equal: the Creator has given us inviolable [absolute] rights, life, liberty and happiness."[6] When it became clear that France was determined to regain Vietnam as a colony, Ho Chi Minh led the resistance movement.

Although Ho Chi Minh was enormously popular – he was known as "Uncle Ho" – his regime became **repressive**. Between 1955 and 1956 he forced peasants to give up their land, even though most had only smallholdings. Thousands were killed during these land reforms. Ho Chi Minh had to admit failure and abandon the policy.

By the time North Vietnam took up arms again in 1959 to support the communist **guerrilla** fighters in South Vietnam, Ho Chi Minh was elderly and less actively involved in politics. He died in 1969, in the midst of the war against the United States. Ho Chi Minh was a significant figure in the battle against colonialism, a battle that would eventually lead to Vietnamese unity and independence.

## Indo-Chinese Communist Party aims

1. To overthrow **imperialism**, the **feudal** system, and the reactionary bourgeoisie [anti-**progressive** ruling class].
2. To win complete independence for Indo-China.
3. To form a government made of workers, peasants, and soldiers.
4. To nationalize the banks … and place them under the control of the proletarian [workers'] government.
5. To confiscate [seize] the agricultural estates owned by the imperialists and bourgeois reactionaries in order to share them out among the poor peasants.

The Party also called for an eight-hour working day, democracy, education for all, and equality between men and women.[7]

# ENTER THE USA

After the defeat of France at Dien Bien Phu and the division of Vietnam, the United States gave support to the South Vietnamese government of Ngo Dinh Diem, based in the city of Saigon. It wanted to prevent the South from turning communist as the North had done. Many in the South agreed with this aim. Yet Diem's regime was dishonest from the start: in 1955 he **rigged** the election to confirm his role as head of state. Although his regime was inefficient and repressive, the United States provided it with aid until 1963, when Diem could no longer control the unrest among the population.

The landowners and the Catholic minority backed Diem, but his policies were unpopular with most people. Diem uprooted peasants from their land to fortified villages called agrovilles in order to prevent communists from entering and attracting support. He introduced a law that allowed him to sentence anyone thought to be a communist to life imprisonment or execution. Diem also expanded the Army of the Republic of Vietnam (ARVN). In response to these measures, increasing numbers of people turned to the communists.

## PREPARING FOR BATTLE

Although many in North Vietnam believed they should focus on building their own state, there was mounting pressure to help free South Vietnam from Diem's harsh rule. There was also a desire to unite the divided country under communist rule. In 1959 the North opted to use armed struggle to overthrow Diem. The North Vietnamese began to smuggle arms down the Ho Chi Minh Trail through Cambodia and Laos to South Vietnam and, in 1960, North Vietnam introduced military **conscription** to build a strong army.

In 1960 the National Liberation Front for South Vietnam (NLF) was formed. It brought together communists and non-communists in the South. Its military wing, with full-time soldiers and guerrilla forces, was the People's Liberation Armed Forces (PLAF). It fought Diem's army for control of South Vietnam.

## BIOGRAPHY

### Ngo Dinh Diem 1901–1963

**BORN:** Quang Binh province, northern Vietnam

**ROLE:** President of the Republic of Vietnam (South Vietnam)

Born into a Catholic family, Ngo Dinh Diem served as Emperor Bao Dai's minister of the interior in 1933. In 1945 he was captured by communist forces and invited to join the new government in the North. He refused and moved abroad.

Ngo Dinh Diem returned to Vietnam in 1954 to become prime minister under Bao Dai. He defeated Bao Dai in 1955 and installed himself as president of the Republic of Vietnam. Diem refused to hold free elections and heavily repressed the growing NLF movement. The United States withdrew support from Diem in 1963, and he was **assassinated** by South Vietnamese army officers.

**DID YOU KNOW?** Bao Dai was not keen to appoint Diem in 1954 but explained later that "in that moment there was no better choice".[1]

## JFK AND VIETNAM

In January 1961, as NLF opposition to Diem was developing in South Vietnam, John F. Kennedy became president of the United States. President Eisenhower warned his successor: "If we let South Vietnam fall [to communism], the next domino Laos, Cambodia, Burma and on down the Subcontinent will fall."[2] This was the domino theory: the fear that once one country fell to communism, its neighbour would follow and the process would continue like dominoes toppling over. There was ample evidence that this could occur. For instance, after the Russian Revolution of 1917, revolutions erupted in several other countries, including Hungary, Germany, China, and Korea (although these revolutions were short-lived and the countries did not turn communist at this time).

Early in his presidency, events in Cuba gave Kennedy grave cause for concern. In April 1961, the United States supported Cuban **exiles** in the Bay of Pigs invasion, an attempt to spark an uprising in Cuba and overthrow the communist government of Fidel Castro. It failed, and Cuba remained communist.

△ These women and girls are planting rice in South Vietnam in the 1960s. Diem failed to bring about land reform and imposed harsh taxes on ordinary people like them.

Fearing another foreign policy fiasco, Kennedy sent more advisers to South Vietnam and continued to provide military and economic aid to the government. US aircraft began to spray chemicals to strip trees of their leaves to make it harder for the North Vietnamese to secretly shift weapons and supplies to their southern allies (see pages 16–17).

## THE APPEAL OF THE NLF

However, the NLF continued to grow in power. By 1963 it had taken over control of territory containing up to half of the southern population, and brought in its own rules.[3] In contrast to the Diem regime, the NLF brought in taxation that was based on the peasants' ability to pay. It introduced moderate land reform in areas under its control, avoiding the mistakes of the drastic reforms in the North in the mid-1950s (see page 11). To avoid upsetting landlords, the NLF redistributed land only where holdings were greater than 100 hectares (250 acres).[4] A communist activist in the South explained how the NLF appealed to villagers: "they say: 'the peasants are the main force of the revolution; if they follow the [Communist] Party, they will become masters of the countryside and owners of their land', and that scratches the peasants right where they itch."[5]

## South Vietnam must not fall

As early as November 1961, the US government was considering sending troops to South Vietnam. Secretary of Defence Robert McNamara and Secretary of State Dean Rusk made these recommendations to President Kennedy:

*"The United States should commit itself to the clear objective of preventing the fall of South Viet-Nam to Communism. The basic means for accomplishing this objective must be to put the Government of South Viet-Nam into a position to win its own war against the guerrillas. We must insist that Government itself take the measures necessary for that purpose in exchange for large-scale United States assistance in the military, economic and political fields ... We should be prepared to introduce United States combat forces if that should become necessary for success."[6]*

# AGENT ORANGE

The NLF guerrillas relied on the thickly forested areas of Vietnam, Laos, and Cambodia for camouflage. They carried out attacks and then disappeared rapidly into the vegetation. Their supporters **covertly** transported equipment down the Ho Chi Minh Trail to South Vietnam.

In 1961, US forces embarked on Operation Ranch Hand to destroy the foliage. As well as demolishing the guerrillas' camouflage, they aimed to ruin Vietnamese agriculture in NLF-controlled areas to deprive the guerrillas of food. Although many farmers simply wanted to get on with their lives, regardless of who ruled them, the official US attitude appeared to be, "You are either with us or against us". The army therefore targeted the entire population of these areas. Aircraft sprayed Agent Orange, which contained the chemical dioxin, over the forests and crops of South Vietnam, and the Ho Chi Minh Trail in particular. By 1971 about 2.2 million hectares (5.5 million acres) of land had been sprayed at least once[7] – an area roughly equivalent to 13,000 average US farms today. Dioxin is toxic even in tiny quantities.

△ The photograph at the top was taken in 1965 before this forest was sprayed with Agent Orange. The second was taken in 1970, after the spraying. The black areas are the only trees that are left.

## A TOXIC LEGACY

The poisonous chemicals not only killed trees and crops. They also flowed into the water, entering the ecosystem and the human food chain. Vietnamese people exposed to Agent Orange developed skin diseases and cancer, as did those US, Australian, and New Zealand soldiers who had been exposed to it – especially those who had worked for Operation Ranch Hand. Vietnamese women suffered from womb cancer and large numbers gave birth to deformed and disabled babies. Some had no arms or legs, or organs on the outside of the body, or learning disabilities. Dioxin still contaminates the environment today in 28 "hotspots" in Vietnam, damaging food supplies and health.[8]

After US soldiers returned home, some of their children were also born with serious birth defects. In 1979 US **veterans** filed a lawsuit against the companies that had produced Agent Orange. In 1985 the veterans won compensation for their suffering.

## A CONTROVERSIAL DECISION

Was it right to use chemical warfare? The government argued that it was an economical way of depriving the guerrillas of camouflage and food. Others countered that the use of poisonous chemicals was unjustifiable under any circumstances.

### "Spray the town"

Some US "ranch hands" who sprayed Agent Orange sang this song to the tune of Jerry Livingston's 1955 song "Wake the Town and Tell the People". Here are two verses:

*Spray the town and kill the people,*
*Spray them with your poison gas;*
*Watch them throwing up their breakfast*
*As you make your second pass.*

*Get the spray pumps working double*
*Slightly offset for the breeze;*
*See the children in convulsions [seizures] –*
*And besides it kills the trees.* [9]

## TERROR IN SOUTH VIETNAM

The NLF adopted more progressive policies in the areas under its control than the South Vietnamese government. However, it acted ruthlessly against its enemies in other parts of South Vietnam. In the early 1960s, the NLF killed around 6,000 local officials and up to 25,000 civilians.[10] During this period, Diem also stepped up his use of terror against civilians, particularly in reaction to the Buddhist demonstrations.

## BUDDHISTS TAKE TO THE STREETS

In 1963, Buddhist protests emerged as part of the campaign against Diem's repressive government. The Buddhists wanted religious freedom and legal equality with Catholics.[11] In June around 300 Buddhist nuns and monks marched in Saigon, led by 76-year-old Thich Quang Duc in a car. The procession stopped at a busy junction and Thich Quang Duc sat on a cushion in the road. Another monk poured petrol over him. Then the seated monk struck a match and set himself on fire. US journalist David Halberstam later described how, "Flames were coming from a human being; his body was slowly withering and shrivelling up, his head blackening and charring."[12] This extraordinary form of political protest had been practised in extreme circumstances by Buddhists for centuries, but it came as a great shock to Western observers.

△ The Buddhist monk Thich Quang Duc burned himself to death in an act of protest.

After this dramatic **self-immolation** the Buddhist campaign, based at Xa Loi temple in Saigon, grew in strength. There were five further self-immolations. The movement spread to the wider population, becoming a broader anti-Diem campaign. In August 1963, the president responded by sending in the army to raid the temple and arrest the protesters. He also banned public gatherings and closed secondary schools and universities. The regime was in crisis.

The United States realized it could do nothing to bolster Diem's authority. It backed a military **coup** against him in November 1963, during which he was murdered. Three weeks later, President Kennedy was himself assassinated in the United States.

## WOULD KENNEDY HAVE DISENGAGED FROM VIETNAM?

Debate has raged over whether, if Kennedy had lived, he would have disengaged from Vietnam rather than committing US troops. William Pfaff, author of several books on international politics, has argued that Kennedy had made a decision to withdraw US involvement. However, biographer Kai Bird contends that: "it is probably safe to say that President Kennedy had not made up his mind about Vietnam before he was assassinated."[13]

### Provoking Buddhists

The French colonists had favoured Catholics and **discriminated** against Buddhists. Diem followed the same policy. In May 1963, this unfairness sparked off a protest movement. The deputy province chief, Major Dang Xi, told Buddhists they were not allowed to fly flags to celebrate the birthday of the Buddha. When they gathered in front of the city's radio station to listen to a broadcast by Tri Quang, a Buddhist leader, the radio station director cancelled the broadcast. Then Major Xi called in the army to disperse the crowd. Soldiers fired on the peaceful gathering; a woman and eight children died in the chaos. The incident outraged Buddhists, and their protests rapidly multiplied.

# THE US MILITARY GOES IN

The replacement of Diem did not solve the political crisis in South Vietnam. The NLF continued to gain ground during 1964, and the North's military forces were also building up strength. Lyndon Johnson, the new US president, believed communists would conquer South Vietnam. Determined to prevent this, he sent in troops, believing that a strong US force, combined with massive bombing, would compel the North to withdraw its support for the NLF.

## AGGRESSION ON THE HIGH SEAS

In August 1964, a clash took place between North Vietnamese patrol boats and the US destroyer, the *Maddox*, in the Gulf of Tonkin. Two days later, the *Maddox* and the *Turner Joy* claimed that they were under attack. Based on the evidence available at the time, Johnson obtained **Congress** support for direct military action against Vietnam. Preparations were made for a bombing campaign.

### The Gulf of Tonkin incident

According to US Assistant Secretary of State William Bundy, President Johnson had discussed the need for a Congress resolution to attack Vietnam in May 1964. These discussions were abandoned. The clashes in August of that year forced the issue; the first attack on the *Maddox* certainly did occur, although at the time it was unclear whether the second attack had taken place. (It was later proved that it had not.) Johnson failed to mention to Congress that the *Maddox* and the *Turner Joy* had been engaged in covert operations against the North. At the same time, he used the two attacks as an excuse to obtain Congress support for military action. If Johnson had adopted a different approach, could he have avoided the descent into war?

In the North, military commander General Nguyen Chi Thanh favoured a major confrontation with the United States. From September 1964, PAVN troops started to move down the Ho Chi Minh Trail to support the NLF. China had pledged to support the North, and the Soviet Union also promised military aid. By the end of 1964, China had agreed to send a large number of troops to North Vietnam to free up PAVN forces to defend the southern frontier.

## FLAMING DART AND ROLLING THUNDER

The stage was set for an escalation of the conflict. In February 1965, NLF guerrillas attacked US military bases in South Vietnam. In response, Johnson ordered Operation Flaming Dart, an aerial bombing campaign against military targets and communications centres in the North. A few weeks later, Operation Rolling Thunder began, targeting North Vietnamese ports, railway lines, and bridges. The bombing of North Vietnam would continue on and off until US forces were withdrawn in 1973.

| US & South Vietnamese allies | NLF & North Vietnamese allies |
|---|---|
| US Army | National Liberation Front of South Vietnam (NLF, also known as the Viet Cong or VC): a mass organization including communists |
| Small forces from Australia, New Zealand, and South Korea | People's Liberation Armed Forces (PLAF): anti-government army and guerrillas from South Vietnam |
| The Army of the Republic of Vietnam (ARVN) | People's Army of Vietnam (PAVN): the North Vietnamese army |

△ This table shows the forces in Vietnam and the side on which they fought.

## THE TROOPS GO IN

President Johnson decided to send ground troops in to Vietnam. Many young men (and some women) volunteered, but others (100,000 in 1964) were **drafted** and forced to go and fight. The draft was extremely unpopular in the United States, and many people tried to avoid it. The powerful impact of the draft on US attitudes to the war is discussed more fully on pages 44–45 and 47.

In March 1965, the United States landed the first combat troops in South Vietnam. General Westmoreland hoped that his soldiers, with their superior firepower, would kill so many of their opponents that they would not be able to replace their losses and would surrender.

The United States experienced some early successes in **conventional** battles. For example, in October 1965 its forces defeated the North Vietnamese army in the Ia Drang Valley, in the Central Highlands. However, conventional warfare would not be the major arena of struggle and more forces would be needed. By this time, 35,000 men were being drafted to Vietnam every month.

The US forces attempted to grind down the enemy through "search and destroy" missions: they tried to find and kill suspected guerrillas in a particular area. Often the fighters had disappeared, and civilians were killed instead. Once the troops had left the area, the guerrillas returned. Rather than destroying NLF forces, this killing of Vietnamese civilians fuelled support for the resistance.

## GUERRILLA WARFARE

The guerrilla forces rapidly multiplied in South Vietnam. In the early years of the war, the Vietnamese had a huge advantage in guerrilla warfare. They knew the terrain and many were trained to survive in the rainforests. They had experience of the war against the French, too. Their tactic was to hide, wait, and ambush US soldiers. They would then escape into the forest and blend into the community.

In contrast, US soldiers were trained for conventional warfare, but were not used to the Vietnamese climate or survival in the forests. Large numbers fell ill with serious diseases, such as malaria and dysentery.

Search and destroy missions involved, "trudging day after day, with heavy packs, from one spot on a map to another looking in vain for an elusive enemy".[1] Later in the war, the US Army adopted the far more effective guerrilla tactics of the NLF.

General Westmoreland tried to meet the challenge in Vietnam with greater troop numbers. These more than doubled from 1965 to 1966, and increased further in 1967. Combat casualties rose accordingly, reaching more than 16,000 in 1967.[2] Even so, the United States could not crush the Vietnamese resistance.

## Living in a tunnel

Tran Thi Gung was the only woman in her NLF unit, which was based in Cu Chi. This was an extensive tunnel network near Saigon where guerrillas hid for protection.

"When GIs discovered tunnel openings they dynamited them, but the tunnels were so deep and had so many twists and turns, they couldn't do too much damage. It was like an underground maze. Most of the tunnels were just wide enough to crawl through … Most of the time we lived in the dark … Usually we didn't have to stay underground for more than a few hours at a time. After all, we had to be above ground to fight, right? But one time I was stuck in a tunnel for seven days and seven nights while the Americans were constantly bombing us."[3]

You can find out more at: http://news.bbc.co.uk/1/hi/world/asia-pacific/720577.stm

◁ This recent photograph shows a soldier standing in the cramped Cu Chi tunnels.

# WILLIAM EHRHART

When William Ehrhart first joined the US Army, he had a romantic vision of the military, stimulated by film heroes. He calls this the "John Wayne syndrome". He thought Vietnam would be like the World War II films he had seen, with women and children rushing out on to the streets to greet their liberators.

## CORDON-AND-SEARCH

Once he arrived in Vietnam, he realized that the intention of US missions did not match the reality. During "cordon-and-search" missions from 1965, the soldiers were supposed to enter villages, offering food and medical care, while looking for NLF members. In practice, as Ehrhart explained, "We would go through a village before dawn, rousting everybody out of bed, and kicking down doors and dragging them out if they didn't move fast enough. They all had underground bunkers inside their huts to protect themselves against bombing and shelling. But to us the bunkers were Viet Cong hiding places, and we'd blow them up with dynamite – and blow up the huts too."[4]

South Vietnamese police officers would then select villagers to be taken for questioning. These people might be beaten, tortured, or taken to jail. Ehrhart described the effect of these "routine" missions: "At the end of

△ These US soldiers are looking for NLF members.

the day, the villagers would be turned loose. Their homes had been wrecked, their chickens killed, their rice confiscated – and if they weren't pro-Viet Cong before we got there, they sure as hell were by the time we left."[5]

## GROWING DOUBTS

Even though Ehrhart had volunteered to enlist, he began to question the war in Vietnam, as did many other US soldiers: "Maybe we Americans weren't the guys in white hats, riding white horses. Maybe we shouldn't be in Vietnam … Still, it never occurred to me to lay down my rifle and quit. Instead you develop a survival mentality. You stop thinking about what you're doing, and you count days. I knew that I was in Vietnam for 395 days, and if I was still alive at the end of those 395 days, I'd go home and forget the whole thing."[6] However, Ehrhart did not forget Vietnam when he went home. Instead, he eventually joined the anti-war movement.

## BIOGRAPHY

### William Ehrhart

BORN: Roaring Spring, Pennsylvania, USA, 1948

ROLE: Soldier and anti-war campaigner

William Ehrhart joined the Marines in 1966 and was posted to Vietnam the following year. During his first tour of duty, he took part in many combat operations and was injured by **shrapnel** from a rocket in the battle for Hue during the Tet Offensive (see page 26). He left Vietnam in 1968 but continued to serve as a soldier. After leaving the army in 1972, he joined Vietnam Veterans Against the War and later worked as a teacher and writer. He has published many poems, essays, and accounts of his wartime experiences.

DID YOU KNOW? Ehrhart was only 18 years old when he joined the Marines. The average age of the US soldiers who fought in Vietnam was just 19.

# ONGOING WAR

The NLF launched the Tet Offensive in 1968. They attacked cities, towns, and villages throughout South Vietnam. The NLF hoped the offensive would spur an uprising against the government of US-backed Nguyen van Thieu. The plan failed, and the war dragged on for a further five years.

▷ This map shows where the NLF carried out their main attacks during the Tet Offensive.

## THE TET OFFENSIVE

During Tet, fierce battles raged across the South. The NLF seized and held Hue for almost three weeks. Elsewhere, the US and South Vietnamese troops forced them to withdraw within a few days. The population did not rise up to support the NLF, and casualties were high. It is estimated that the United States lost 2,000 soldiers, the South Vietnamese 4,000, and the North Vietnamese 40,000.[1]

Despite the defeat of the North and the NLF, Tet sent shockwaves through US society. General William Westmoreland had promised that victory was in sight, yet the extensive television coverage of battles in Saigon and Hue showed that the United States faced a strong enemy.

In March 1968, it was reported that Westmoreland had asked for 206,000 additional troops for Vietnam.[2] The public realized that the situation in Vietnam was dire. Anti-war protests increased. In an abrupt policy shift, Johnson announced that he would not commit more troops, the bombing of North Vietnam would end, and he would request peace talks.

### Stalemate in Vietnam

The well-respected television news presenter Walter Cronkite toured South Vietnam after the Tet Offensive and called for negotiations. The fact that such an important and respected reporter believed the United States should end the war had a significant impact on public opinion and even the government.

*"To say that we are mired in **stalemate** seems the only realistic, yet unsatisfactory, conclusion ... [I]t is increasingly clear to this reporter that the only rational way out then will be to negotiate."*[3]

You can read Cronkite's broadcast from 27 February 1968 here: https://facultystaff.richmond.edu/~ebolt/history398/cronkite_1968.html

## STALEMATE IN PARIS

North Vietnam agreed to enter negotiations, and in May 1968 peace talks began in Paris. North Vietnam wanted a full US withdrawal from South Vietnam and a new **coalition** government including the NLF. The United States insisted it would withdraw only if the North Vietnamese did, too, and would not consider the replacement of Thieu's government. The talks quickly stalled. Then in November 1968, Richard Nixon won the US presidential election with the promise that he would achieve "peace with honour" in Vietnam.

**BIOGRAPHY**

**Richard Nixon** 1913–1994

BORN: California, USA

ROLE: President of the United States, 1969–1974

Nixon was an active anti-communist. He was elected to the House of Representatives in 1946. Serving as vice-president from 1952–1960, he lost the presidential election in 1960, but won in 1968, promising that he had a "secret plan" to end the war. Although he reduced the number of US troops, he resumed the bombing of North Vietnam and launched invasions of Cambodia and Laos. Critics argued that these actions achieved nothing. In 1973, the year the war finally ended, the Watergate scandal came to a head. It was revealed that Nixon had carried out illegal activities against his political opponents in the US. He resigned in disgrace in 1974.

DID YOU KNOW? It is thought that Nixon became so angry about the US failure to defeat North Vietnam that in 1972 he even considered using a nuclear bomb.

## VIETNAMIZATION

In 1969 Nixon reduced the number of US troops while providing aid to allow an increase in ARVN forces. This became known as "Vietnamization". The number of ARVN troops rose rapidly from

△ South Vietnamese ARVN troops run to board a helicopter for a mission in the Mekong Delta.

850,000 when Nixon took office to more than 1 million.[4] The United States provided vast quantities of weapons to South Vietnam as well. Nixon hoped that the ARVN forces would be able to counter the threat from the NLF and the North.

However, the army suffered from a lack of morale. The South Vietnamese were not as motivated as their northern counterparts, and **desertion** was a problem. The ARVN feared the scaling down of US forces indicated that its powerful ally would soon leave the small nation alone to its fate.

## OPERATION PHOENIX

While expanding the ARVN, the United States also initiated Operation Phoenix to arrest and interrogate suspected NLF guerrillas; most of those captured were killed. However, the programme suffered from inefficiency and abuse. Village authorities (officials who ruled at village level) had to fulfil monthly quotas, so they classed anyone killed as an NLF member. Even so, after the war, senior NLF figures admitted that Operation Phoenix did wipe out many of their members. Overall, however, Nixon's policies did not succeed. By 1970 he and his national security adviser Henry Kissinger (see page 35), had planned a dangerous new venture.

## MILITARY TECHNOLOGY

On the ground, US soldiers were outnumbered by NLF forces by three or four to one.[5] The United States' strength lay in its industrial power; it had emerged from World War II the strongest nation "because American industry had mobilized more might, more bangs and bucks, than any other country on earth".[6] During the Vietnam War, the United States developed state-of-the-art technologies in the hope of beating the Vietnamese through sheer military might. The Vietnamese resistance relied on Soviet technology, which was cheaper but less sophisticated.

### The terror of a B-52 raid

Senior NLF official Truong Nhu Tang remembered the fear of living with B-52 raids "day in, day out, for years on end. From a kilometre away, the sonic roar of the B-52 explosions tore eardrums, leaving many of the jungle dwellers permanently deaf ... Any hit within half a kilometre would collapse the walls of an unreinforced bunker, burying alive the people cowering inside."[8]

The bombing of North and South Vietnam, and later Cambodia and Laos, was an essential element of US policy. From 1965 the US Air Force began using giant B-52 bombers to drop anti-personnel cluster bombs. These were known as "mother bombs" because they exploded in the air, releasing hundreds of "baby bombs" that blew up to expel thousands of flesh-cutting pellets. Smaller jets were used to **strafe** people on the ground. The Americans also used napalm, particularly in Laos. This jellied petrol was dropped in bombs from planes to set fire to vegetation and attack the enemy. It stuck to people's flesh and caused horrific burns. Most of the deaths in Vietnam, Cambodia, and Laos were a result of aerial warfare.[7]

As the war progressed, the United States developed sophisticated remote-control techniques to detect the enemy. Ground sensors detected movement and transmitted signals remotely to computers, which activated aircraft bombing of the target. Helicopter gunships with infra-red scopes were developed to detect targets in the dark and follow them on television monitors.

North Vietnamese soldiers at an anti-aircraft position watch out for US planes.

## NORTH VIETNAMESE TACTICS

The North lacked such advanced technology. It obtained MiG 17 planes from the Soviet Union but had fewer aircraft than its opponents. Although smaller and easier to manoeuvre, MiGs were slower and less heavily armed than the US aircraft. The North Vietnamese used them in "hit and run" raids to try to break up large formations of US bombers and fighter planes. They also focused on employing Soviet early-warning radar systems to track enemy aircraft. They would try to destroy them with anti-aircraft guns before they released their deadly load. Surface-to-air missiles (SAMs), also guided by radar, were used to target US aircraft, too.

### Daisy cutters

It sounds harmless, but the BLU-82, or "daisy cutter", was in fact a massive bomb of 6,800 kilograms (15,000 pounds). It could blast a 79-metre (260-foot) wide space in vegetation to allow helicopters to land. They were first used in Vietnam in 1970.[9]

# THE HELICOPTER

Vietnamese guerrillas had the advantage of mobility and were able to launch surprise attacks on US forces. The Americans needed to match this flexibility. They opted to use helicopters, which could be flown into forests and urban areas alike and landed in small spaces. As General Westmoreland said, "The most spectacular development was the coming of age of the helicopters. It saved innumerable [countless] lives through air evacuation. It gave us a battlefield mobility that we never dreamed of years previously."[10] Indeed, the Vietnam War is known as the first helicopter war.

## A VERSATILE VEHICLE

Helicopters had many uses. They carried troops and weapons and flew the seriously wounded to hospital. Giant transport helicopters, such as the Chinook, were specially developed for moving large numbers of troops in and out of the battlefield. The Bell UH-1 Iroquois, known as a "Huey", eventually became the most popular helicopter for this job. Helicopters also supported ground troops. Helicopter gunships such as the HueyCobra could be loaded up with rockets, **grenade** launchers and guided missiles, with machine guns fitted in the nose, belly pod,

The US soldier manning the door gun of this Huey helicopter opens fire on a target below, 1968.

and open doorway. Formations of up to 40 of these "flying tanks" sped through the skies at up to 310 kilometres (195 miles) per hour[11] to launch combat assaults. In urban areas, soldiers could fire rockets, missiles, and bullets from the air or land on the top of buildings close to a battle site.

## LIMITATIONS

However, helicopters alone could not win a battle. For example, in October 1965, General Westmoreland ordered the 1st Cavalry Division to destroy three regiments of North Vietnamese troops in the Ia Drang river valley in the Central Highlands. Brand new helicopters took **infantrymen** to the battlefield, rescued the wounded, and brought replacements. However, they could not stop their soldiers, once on the ground, from being ambushed by PAVN soldiers.

Additionally, helicopters themselves were vulnerable to attack. As they turned around, the Vietnamese fired machine guns at the low-flying aircraft. They learned how to aim ahead of the helicopter to have the best chance of hitting it, and also which part to shoot to cause the most damage. To overcome this problem, the helicopters flew in large formations for mutual protection. The Vietnamese were highly successful at shooting down "choppers" with Soviet surface-to-air missiles (SAMs).

Helicopters were prone to break down and it was hard to maintain them in wartime conditions. Overall, the United States lost 4,869 helicopters during the war, 53 per cent to enemy fire and the rest to accidents.[12] Despite the hazards, they proved to be indispensable war vehicles. After the United States' pioneering use of the helicopter in combat, other countries followed suit.

### In praise of helicopters

Former soldier Michael Herr gave this unusual and imaginative description of the helicopter as a "saver-destroyer, provider-waster, right hand-left hand, nimble, fluent, canny and human; hot steel, grease, jungle-saturated canvas webbing, sweat cooling and warming again, cassette rock'n'roll in one ear and door-gun in the other".[13]

## CAMBODIA IN THE CROSSFIRE

In 1969 President Nixon acted on Henry Kissinger's advice to widen the conflict, and ordered the secret bombing of Cambodia. He hoped to hit the Central Office for Southern Vietnam (COSVN), which ran the NLF war effort in South Vietnam. With the bombing of Cambodia, Nixon put his "madman theory" into action – he wanted the North's leaders to believe he was completely unpredictable, like a madman, and would do anything to stop the war.

△ President Nixon (left) with Henry Kissinger in 1972. Kissinger had a huge influence on US foreign policy in Vietnam, Laos, and Cambodia.

The bombing did not destroy the headquarters so, in April 1970, Nixon sent 90,000 US and 40,000 ARVN troops to invade Cambodia.[14] They could not destroy the COSVN either, because it was not a single permanent structure but consisted of activists moving around the forest between makeshift huts.

## WAR SPREADS TO LAOS

In 1971 South Vietnamese troops invaded Laos with US support. They wanted to prevent the North Vietnamese from moving into the South using the Laotian part of the Ho Chi Minh Trail. In this first major test of Vietnamization, the NLF defeated the ARVN, having discovered the invasion plan in advance.

Did the invasions of Cambodia and Laos achieve anything? Nixon claimed it was essential "to protect our men who are in Vietnam and to guarantee the continued success of our withdrawal and the Vietnamization program".[15] Critics countered that the bombings and invasions had killed up to 150,000 Cambodian civilians[16] but did not help to end the Vietnam War.

## BOMBED TO THE PEACE TABLE?

Secret peace talks had been going on since 1969. North Vietnam wanted to strengthen its military position to increase its bargaining power. In 1972, it launched the Easter Offensive with an attack across the partition line into the South. In response, Nixon ordered the sustained bombing of the North. When talks broke down in December, Nixon once again authorized massive air strikes on Hanoi and Haiphong in order to force the North to the table. Known as the "Christmas bombings", bombs rained down for 11 days and nights: 100,000 were dropped on the two cities.[17]

Finally, in January 1973, a **ceasefire** agreement was reached. The US government believed the Christmas bombings had successfully forced the North to the negotiating table. However, the North believed that Nixon had simply run out of time and was keen to settle.

### Henry Kissinger's secret talks

In December 1968, Nixon appointed Kissinger as his national security adviser and together they decided US foreign policy. Henry Kissinger embarked on secret talks with North Vietnam in 1969, which lasted for three years. However, while he discussed peace with his North Vietnamese counterpart Le Duc Tho (who shared Kissinger's obsession with secrecy) he also advised Nixon to increase the bombing of North Vietnam and recommended the expansion of the war into Laos and Cambodia. Indeed, he told the North Vietnamese negotiators that he was a reasonable man who opposed the bombings but that the president was crazy. Kissinger recommended that the North make a deal with him, otherwise Nixon might unleash further violence. When a sticking point arose in the negotiations, Kissinger would tell Nixon to launch new bombings, and return to the North Vietnamese, saying, "See what happens when you don't make your deal with me."[18] Kissinger was playing a double game. Nevertheless, in 1973 he accepted the Nobel Peace Prize for bringing peace to Vietnam; Le Duc Tho declined the honour.

For more information about Kissinger, go to http://news.bbc.co.uk/1/hi/world/americas/2521835.stm

# LIVING THROUGH THE WAR

Wartime experiences varied in the South and North of Vietnam. The South Vietnamese lived in a state of civil conflict as US and government forces battled with the NLF, while North Vietnam had a strong, unified leadership which was supported by the population. Even so, the whole nation endured the trauma of widespread death and devastation, as did the US soldiers fighting there.

## SOUTH VIETNAM

The war in the countryside uprooted peasants from their homes. An estimated 4 million people (25 per cent of the population) became refugees during the war, and many ended up living in vast urban slums.[1] Others, especially in the central coastal provinces and north-west of Saigon, were forced to move when "free-fire zones" were set up. These were zones in areas where the NLF was strong, and where the US army could use unlimited force. For example, in 1967 more than 6,000 villagers were evacuated from Ben Suc village, and the village was devastated by bombs.[2]

Life in the ARVN was harsh. The troops received low wages and, from 1968, their term of service was unlimited. They also did not receive sufficient leave to help their families with farm work. PLAF soldiers had a strictly regimented life but were granted time off to help their families at planting and harvest time. Women played important roles in the PLAF and NLF as fighters and nurses. They were also responsible for their families, so they carried a double burden.

The war had serious economic and social effects. Large numbers lost their livelihoods and poverty increased. The US government poured economic and military aid into South Vietnam but much of it went to the **corrupt** Saigon government. Inflation was sky-high: one estimate showed that the price of rice rose by 1,000 per cent between 1964 and 1972.[3]

## Trinh Cong Son

South Vietnamese songwriter Trinh Cong Son became active against the war in the mid-1960s. The Saigon government banned his songs in 1968, but cassette recordings were secretly circulated and became popular with artists, ARVN soldiers, and even troops on the opposing side. This verse is from "A Lullaby of the Cannons for the Night".

*Thousands of bombs rain down on the village*
*Thousands of bombs rain down on the field*
*And Vietnamese homes burn bright in the hamlet*
*Thousands of trucks with Claymores [mines] and grenades*
*Thousands of trucks enter the cities*
*Carrying the remains of mothers, sisters and brothers.*[4]

Bribes were required for all services, such as acquiring a work permit. A small number of Vietnamese linked to the regime benefited, but the majority did not.

Western culture had a huge impact on South Vietnamese society. Members of the US forces brought pop music and Western clothing, but they also increased the drug problem and encouraged widespread prostitution. On the streets, orphans and people disabled by bombs and mines were forced to beg for money from US soldiers.

▽ These young women in Saigon in 1975 wear Western clothing.

## NORTH VIETNAM

North Vietnam experienced years of bombing, devastation, and hardship. However the leadership, under Le Duan from 1969, worked hard to boost civilian and military morale. A strong set of beliefs, based on fighting for liberation from foreign intervention, bound the population. There was a sense that the North Vietnamese were fighting a "total war" for the survival of their nation. In addition, the government tightly controlled the media to suppress opposition and to promote support for the regime.

△ During the aerial bombing of North Vietnam, US planes destroyed this railway and highway bridge at Ninh Binh, south of Hanoi.

The North Vietnamese had to live with the constant fear of bombing. Between 1965 and 1968, during Operation Rolling Thunder, nearly a million tonnes of bombs were dropped on North Vietnam, killing about 52,000 civilians.[5] The bombers targeted industrial cities, such as Vinh, and hit infrastructure to damage the country's ability to move troops and supplies. The US troops destroyed railway stations and lines, roads, power plants, and bridges. Civilians were continually busy repairing the damage.

To protect civilians, the government evacuated a large proportion of city dwellers to the countryside – up to half the population of major cities at the peak of evacuation in 1968.[6] For those who remained, air-raid shelters were constructed underground, accessible via concrete lids on the main streets.

The rural areas were bombed, too. It is estimated that 70 per cent of the rural North was bombed between 1965 and 1972.[7] People and animals lost their lives, the land was ruined, flood controls and irrigation systems were destroyed, and transport was also disrupted. Living standards fell. There was less food available and many people went hungry between harvests.

## THE WAR EFFORT

A large proportion of the population was directly involved in the fighting; 60 per cent of northern families had a member involved in the war effort, many in the PAVN.[8] Recruits to the PAVN received both military and political training to ensure they understood that they were fighting for their nation's independence.

Women made a huge contribution as fighters and workers. The Australian journalist Wilfred Burchett, who reported from the communist side, found that women made up half of village self-defence units and were trained to handle guns. They also comprised around 70 per cent of the workforce in industry and agriculture.[9] In addition to their war duties, women struggled to feed and clothe their families because of food shortages and the rationing of goods.

### Careful camouflage

During the war, schools were relocated to the countryside along with the children. However, since most rural areas were bombed, the children had to wear camouflage. Wilfred Burchett described the effectiveness of camouflage:

*"It was compulsory for the kids to wear green camouflage when they attended school ... I remember once driving through an area and to my great astonishment the whole field of maize suddenly got to its feet and charged across the road."*[10]

## US SOLDIERS IN VIETNAM

Most GIs were young. From 1969, a lottery selected men between 18 and 26 to be called up for duty. They had to be healthy and not in education. Large numbers of young, middle-class people attended university and could defer (postpone) the draft. Around 80 per cent of those selected to fight were working class;[11] many were African Americans. From 1971 deferments were abolished.

△ An exhausted US soldier, fighting in Vietnam in 1969, takes a welcome rest.

Some soldiers were keen to join up, motivated by patriotism or by a fear of communism. At the time, it was commonly believed that communism was spreading across the globe and threatened the way of life of the United States. Many young people believed they would be heroes fighting a "just war" for freedom. There were a few who relished the excitement of the war, especially the thrill of flying aeroplanes or helicopters. As Jim Soular, flight engineer on enormous CH-47 Chinook helicopters explains, "I loved being on an M-60 machine gun banging away with that thing. God, there was nothing like a combat assault when you went in with twenty, thirty, forty choppers. I mean Hueys everywhere and gunships and CH-47s – just that energy!"[12]

## LOW MORALE AND MISERY

However, many GIs had not chosen to fight in Vietnam and large numbers did not support the war. Morale among the troops declined, particularly from 1968 onwards, as the anti-war movement grew stronger (see page 48). Most of the time, the war was boring and arduous. Army and marine units spent hours trekking through rice fields and forests in sweltering heat, weighed down by up to 32 kilograms (70 pounds) of equipment.[13] The rain soaked them to the skin, while insects and leeches penetrated their clothes. Then, all of a sudden, the monotony would be broken by an ambush, and the soldiers were filled with fear for their lives.

### Casual atrocity

William Ehrhart says, *"One day I shot a woman in a rice field because she was running – just running away from the Americans. And I killed her. Fifty-five or sixty years old, unarmed, and at the time I didn't even think twice about it."* [16]

In this atmosphere, away from the stabilizing influence of family, wives, or girlfriends, many soldiers sought comfort by turning to prostitutes. Around 25 per cent caught sexually transmitted diseases.[14] Drug use was common. In 1970 more than half of GIs smoked hash or opium, while a fifth injected heroin.[15]

## WAR CRIMES

The stress of war led all sides to commit war crimes. The NLF terrorized the opposition in the South, killing police officers, priests, and teachers who refused to co-operate with them. Some US soldiers and Vietnamese fighters committed atrocities against Vietnamese civilians, killing children and raping women. Former soldiers such as Ehrhart (see pages 24–25 and panel above) explain how they committed terrible acts in Vietnam. At the time, they were suffering severe psychological strain from living in constant terror. Every Vietnamese peasant could be an NLF fighter, about to kill them. Often their comrades were killed by guerrillas, who then disappeared, and the US soldiers took out their frustration on civilians.

# THE MY LAI MASSACRE

During February and early March 1968, Charlie Company, a 100-strong US army platoon, suffered several casualties in Son My, in Quang Ngai province. The US soldiers believed that a guerrilla force of around 250 was operating from My Lai, a hamlet in Son My. Intelligence reports indicated that on Tuesdays the women and children left for market by 7.00 a.m. Charlie Company, led by Lieutenant William L. Calley, was ordered to destroy the village after that time.

## SHOOT TO KILL

On Tuesday 16 March, Charlie Company advanced into the village. Their intelligence had been wrong; the village was full of unarmed women, children, and elderly men, who offered no opposition. Nevertheless, Calley ordered his soldiers to go in shooting and to throw grenades into the villagers' dwellings; 30 of them obeyed the instruction. The GIs mowed down all who emerged from their homes. They led groups of civilians to a large ditch and shot them all dead.

Some GIs were more sadistic, stabbing old men with bayonets (long, sharp knives), slaughtering babies, and raping young women before killing them. The soldiers also killed all the livestock, wrecked the houses, and poisoned the wells by throwing in animal carcasses.

The murderous frenzy ended only after Warrant Officer Hugh C. Thompson spotted what was happening from his helicopter, landed in My Lai, and courageously stood up to the soldiers, threatening to shoot them if they killed another Vietnamese person. At 9.00 a.m. the battalion commander arrived and ordered the action to end.[17] Around 500 villagers lay dead.

## DESCENT INTO BARBARISM

How could such horrors occur? Varnado Simpson was 19 years old when he killed around 25 people at My Lai. Later, he related what went through his mind:

*The training came to me and I just started killing. Old men, women, children, water buffaloes, everything. We were told to leave nothing standing. We did what we was [were] told, regardless of whether there were civilians. They was [were] the enemy. Period. Kill.* [18]

Professor Richard Falk commented that the Vietnam War shows how the modern state:

*...can relapse into **barbarism** ... It would be misleading to isolate the awful happening at Son My from the overall conduct of the war [or from] the general line of policy that established a moral climate in which the welfare of Vietnamese civilians is totally disregarded.* [19]

## COURT MARTIAL

In November 1969, Calley was court-martialled (tried by a military court) for the murder of 109 Vietnamese men, women, and children. He was found guilty, spent three days in a military jail, then three and a half years under house arrest (not allowed to leave his home). The 24 other men charged were found not guilty. Once the story was out, attitudes in the United States shifted; millions who had believed the war was misguided but felt it patriotic to support their government began to consider that it was unjust and immoral, and that the government was betraying US values.

### How do we know about My Lai?

Using only official military reports, the *New York Times* reported My Lai as a successful action in which US troops killed 128 Viet Cong. Around 50 US officers knew what had really happened but they covered up the truth. Vietnam veteran Ron Ridenhour had heard rumours of the massacre, and sent the details to senior military and political leaders. The army was eventually put under pressure to investigate, leading to the arrest and court-martialling of Calley.

# THE ANTI-WAR MOVEMENT

Students, trade unions, religious groups, civil rights campaigners, and even many soldiers vehemently opposed the Vietnam War. Opposition grew as the US commitment increased. In the United States, mass demonstrations were held, and young men resisted the draft. In Vietnam, disgruntled GIs refused to follow orders.

## THE MOVEMENT KICKS OFF

The student movement exploded in 1965. In April 25,000 people marched against the war in Washington DC.[1] University students launched the early public protests, but opposition to the war soon grew broader. Resistance became strongest among poorer and less educated Americans – those who were likely to be drafted. Hostility to the war among this group surged even before television images of the horrors of the war influenced society more widely against the conflict.

Protests against the war became international. In 1965 US folk singer Joan Baez performed at a demonstration in London.

## CIVIL RIGHTS AND VIETNAM

Black people played an important role in the movement. During the 1960s, the civil rights movement was struggling to achieve equal rights for African Americans. Meanwhile, the United States claimed to be fighting for freedoms in Vietnam that African Americans did not have in their own country, and sacrificing conscripted black GIs to do so.

Civil rights leader Martin Luther King voiced his anger in April 1967: "[Blacks are dying] in extraordinarily high proportions relative to the rest of the population ... to guarantee liberties in South-East Asia which they had not found in South-West Georgia and East Harlem."[2] He was right: twice as many black soldiers than white were given combat assignments.[3] This injustice drew African Americans to the anti-war movement.

The anti-war demonstrations grew in 1967, bringing together black and white activists. In October 1967, over 50,000 people marched on the Pentagon (US military headquarters near Washington DC), with "white professors marching alongside black Muslims, expressing anger against the draft. Together they chanted 'Hell No, We Won't Go [to Vietnam]'."[4]

Jerry Rubin, an anti-war leader, described the protest as a turning point in the movement. Public opinion was gradually shifting. At the start of 1968, 66 per cent of Americans were "hawks": they thought the United States should increase its military efforts in Vietnam. Just 22 per cent were "doves", favouring a negotiated settlement and withdrawal of troops. Within a few months, the doves outnumbered the hawks.[5]

## The Fulbright Hearings

Senator J. William Fulbright played an important role in bringing opposition to the war into mainstream society. Early in 1966, he began a series of nationally televised **Senate** hearings in which senior government officials debated with critics of the war. Fulbright believed it was wrong for the United States to become involved in the affairs of other countries but should instead, "serve as an example of democracy to the world by the way in which we run our own society".[6]

## MEDIA IMPACT

Reporters had extensive access to the war zones and there was little **censorship** compared to previous or subsequent wars. As historian Christian Appy comments, "From 1965 to 1972 the Vietnam War was such a common feature of nightly television that it became known as the 'living room war'."[7]

Particular events in the war, relayed directly to people's front rooms, catapulted opposition to new heights. The reporting of the Tet Offensive (see pages 26–27) made millions in the United States realize the situation in Vietnam was worse than they had imagined and that it was simply not true that their country was close to victory. Images of napalmed children running away from their villages in terror shocked the nation, and protesters expressed their anger at the brutality of the war being fought in their name.

The military establishment complained that reporters were sabotaging (deliberately damaging) their efforts and reducing public support for the war. However, careful examination of media reports indicates that the majority supported the official US objectives. Thus the media itself did not present a challenge to the war effort. In fact, young activists developed their own alternative, radical newspapers and magazines to expose military atrocities and spread news from North Vietnam and the anti-war movement.

### Body bags

By 1968 a growing number of people in the United States opposed the war because more and more soldiers were returning home dead in body bags – at a rate of at least 1,000 per month.[8] As David Dellinger, a leader of the anti-war movement, commented, "there was a realization that in addition to napalming a peasant civilization 'our sons were being killed'."[9]

## DRAFT RESISTANCE

Another significant element in the US anti-war movement was draft resistance. Activists set up centres to give advice on avoiding recruitment to the army, and people burned draft cards in public protests. Tens of thousands of young men left the country, the majority for Canada. World heavyweight champion boxer Muhammad Ali was an African-American Muslim who refused the draft in 1967, having previously stated, "I ain't got no quarrel with them

Viet Cong" – no Vietnamese had been racist towards him, unlike many US citizens.[10] In punishment, he was stripped of his title and prohibited from continuing as a boxer.

During the entire war, an estimated 250,000 people avoided registering for the draft.[11] Others evaded it by getting married or hastily enrolling in university, which allowed them to defer (delay) enlistment. However, those with the least influence in society found it hardest to resist the call-up, so it tended to be the poorest people, both black and white, who were drafted.

## Draft resistance and desertion

| Avoided the draft through student and occupational deferments and other factors | 15 million[12] |
|---|---|
| Went to prison for openly resisting the draft on grounds of conscience | 3,250[13] |
| Deserted from the US Army (1968–1975) | more than 93,000[14] |

△ These protesters are burning their draft cards in 1968.

## THE GI REVOLT

Protests and draft resistance encouraged the anti-war revolt within the army. In the United States, radicals set up meetings and anti-war newspapers for their military base. During the war, there were about 300 such newspapers.[15] Challenges to military authority were linked to the civil rights movement, too. African-American soldiers, angered by racism in society and within the army, established **black nationalist** groups on bases to promote their struggle for equality with whites. They also opposed the war. For example, one meeting at a base in Heidelberg, Germany, in July 1970 demanded equal rights within the army and the withdrawal of US troops from South-East Asia.[16]

In Vietnam itself, soldiers began to reject missions. Company scout Mike Beaman recalls:

*We used to refuse certain missions because we thought they were brutal ... if I felt that we were going to have a confrontation and shoot people for no reason at all ... I'd say 'No ... I'm going this way. You, officer, can go that way, but the other people will follow me.'*[17]

This was known as "combat refusal", and the offender could be punished by court martial.

▽ This protest by veterans of the war took place in 1971.

From 1969 officers who insisted on sending their men on dangerous patrols were at risk of "fragging" – the GIs would throw a fragmentation bomb into their tent. According to Congressional data, there were 730 "fragging" incidents, in which 83 officers were murdered, as well as numerous other assaults on officers.[18] These crimes often went unpunished. In the chaotic circumstances of jungle warfare, it was hard to prove the offence had occurred.

Back in the United States, veterans who had returned from Vietnam disillusioned with the conflict began their own rebellion. In 1967 they formed Vietnam Veterans Against the War (VVAW), joining demonstrations and holding their own protests. In April 1971, for example, 2,000 veterans marched to Congress in Washington DC in their army uniforms to publicly throw away their medals. The actions of the veterans were significant because they showed that the peace movement was not motivated by feelings against the GIs but instead the desire to save them by ending the war.

## DID THE ANTI-WAR MOVEMENT SUCCEED?

Surprisingly, the movement's leaders felt it had a minimal impact. One leader, Eugene McCarthy, claimed that Nixon was going to pull out of Vietnam anyway because the United States was losing. However, other observers believed the movement placed pressure on Nixon to withdraw troops and cut funds for the war, thus hastening the conclusion of the conflict.

## The anti-war movement

**March 1965**: First anti-war **teach-in** at the University of Michigan.[19]

**April 1965**: Anti-war demonstration in Washington DC attracts 25,000.[20]

**April 1967**: Martin Luther King, the leader of the US civil rights movement, publicly declares his opposition to the war.[21]

**November 1969**: 250,000 people demonstrate against the war in Washington DC.[22]

**May 1970**: At a protest against the US invasion of Cambodia at Kent State University, Ohio (see pages 50–51), the **National Guard** shoot dead four students.

**May 1971**: Vietnam Veterans Against the War demonstrate in Massachusetts.

# THE KENT STATE UNIVERSITY PROTEST

When President Nixon announced the invasion of Cambodia on 29 April 1970, anti-war protests broke out across the nation. Like others, the students at Kent State University in Ohio were incensed that Nixon was spreading the war rather than ending it.

Two days after Nixon's announcement, 2,000 protesters set fire to the Reserve Officers Training Corps building on the university campus. The National Guard (a part-time reserve army) was called in to restore order. On 4 May around 1,000 students attended a rally. A few angry students threw rocks at the National Guard, and, to the shock of the assembled crowd, the Guardsmen retaliated first with tear gas and then with live fire.

## SHOT TO DEATH

Historian Kenneth Heinemann described the shootings:

*The soldiers ... turned and fired into the crowd. In thirteen seconds the Guardsmen expended sixty-one rounds. A few hundred feet away in the parking lot, Alison Krause fell mortally wounded. Canfora took a bullet in the wrist and Grace, shot in the foot, writhed in agony. Loaded onto an ambulance, Grace watched as medical attendants pulled a blanket over Sandy Scheuer's head.*[23]

Four students were dead and nine others wounded.

Afterwards, the Guardsmen argued that they were in fear for their lives. However, many experts contended that the students were unarmed and presented no immediate danger to the soldiers.

△ Protesters at Kent State University scattered when the National Guard fired tear gas at them.

## DARK DAYS

The number of deaths was clearly not significant compared to the killings in Vietnam, but shooting student demonstrators was a new outrage. Across the country, students protested at the killings.

Nixon was deeply affected by the events, writing later that "Those few days after Kent State were among the darkest of my presidency."[24] Many delegations visited the White House to voice their opposition to his actions. As John Ehrlichman, Nixon's domestic affairs adviser, recalls, the visitors declared, "We don't like what's happening in Cambodia, and we don't like what happened at Kent State ... and why can't we just get out [of Vietnam]?"[25]

Under intense pressure, Nixon backed down. On 30 June he withdrew US troops from Cambodia, although he ordered the ARVN to continue their work. The military leaders were furious. It seemed to them that "government policy was made in the streets".[26] It did indeed appear that the events at an Ohio university had greatly influenced government policy.

# VIETNAM UNITED

After the January 1973 ceasefire, the United States still supported the South Vietnamese government. Yet within two years, the South fell to the communists.

## VIETNAMESE GOVERNMENT IN CRISIS

Although the United States continued to provide aid to South Vietnam, this decreased from $2.3 billion in 1973 to $1 billion in 1974.[1] Since Thieu's regime was weak and corrupt, leading members of the ruling group siphoned off much of this aid for their own benefit. For example, a US survey in 1974 found that commanders were robbing army payrolls (wages) while more than 90 per cent of the soldiers were not receiving enough pay.[2] Severe economic problems exacerbated the difficulties. The world oil crisis of 1973 led to soaring oil prices, inflation reached 90 per cent, and 3-4 million people were unemployed.[3] Many people lost their jobs with US companies that had left when the army withdrew.

These South Vietnamese are fleeing Saigon in April 1975.

## "You did not win"

In his resignation speech, Thieu accused the United States of letting down South Vietnam. "The Americans have asked us to do an impossible thing ... You have asked us to do something you failed to do with half a million powerful troops and skilled commanders and with nearly $300 billion in expenditures over six long years. If I do not say that you were defeated by the communists in Vietnam I must modestly say that you did not win either."[4]

Yet Thieu was convinced the United States would come to his rescue if North Vietnam attacked South Vietnam. In January 1973, Nixon had promised him in a secret letter, "You have my assurance ... that we will respond with full force should the settlement be violated by the North Vietnamese".[5] However, during 1973, Nixon was being brought to account by Congress for the covert bombing of Cambodia, and in 1974 the Watergate scandal forced him to resign (see page 28). The new government was not prepared to commit military forces to South Vietnam.

## COMMUNIST VICTORY

Meanwhile, the North was determined to unify the country, and NLF forces were multiplying in South Vietnam. North Vietnamese and PLAF troops fought the South Vietnamese and seized territory in the Central Highlands, the Mekong Delta, and in late 1974, two provincial capitals close to the Cambodian border. The United States did not intervene militarily and the North Vietnamese realized they would not return. The PAVN and PLAF pushed on to take further cities. In March 1975, the assault on Saigon commenced.

On 21 April, Thieu resigned the presidency and soon fled the country. The United States ordered the evacuation of all its personnel. Panic broke out among the South Vietnamese who had been associated with the Americans, terrified they would be murdered by the North Vietnamese. In desperation, they scrambled for places on US ships or helicopters. On 30 April, the North Vietnamese forces took Saigon. The Republic of Vietnam was no more.

## REUNIFICATION

There was jubilation in Hanoi. North Vietnamese leader Le Duan made a speech in May 1975 celebrating victory and reflecting his belief that world capitalism was failing and Vietnamese socialism would prevail. Southern fears that those linked with the Thieu regime would be massacred proved to be unfounded. Senior North Vietnamese journalist, Bui Tin, attempted to reassure the people of the South, writing "You have nothing to fear. Between Vietnamese, there are no victors and no vanquished. Only the Americans have been beaten."[6]

However, the South Vietnamese who had worked for the government found the defeat a harsh experience. Vu Thi Kim Vinh, the daughter of an ARVN officer, heard a Northerner on the radio the day after the communists conquered Saigon. She said: "He humiliated us by saying that we had been the servants and the dogs of the American government ... We were very hurt to hear that."[7] The new government sent hundreds of thousands of Southerners to **re-education camps** – mostly those associated with the Saigon administration, but also people seen as a danger to the new regime. Others found they were denied jobs because of their links with the old government.

▽ On 30 April 1975, North Vietnamese soldiers entered Saigon in triumph.

## REMODELLING THE COUNTRY

The North remodelled South Vietnam on Northern political principles. The education system was overhauled to incorporate communist ideas. The government took over some major industries and utilities but allowed Southerners to continue to run their businesses and farms. In 1976 the country was unified as the Socialist Republic of Vietnam.

**Amerasians** who remained in Vietnam suffered relentless discrimination. Eventually, in 1987, Congress passed the Amerasian Homecoming Act, which permitted mothers and immediate family members to move to the United States with their Amerasian children.[8]

## The *bui doi* ("dust of life")

During the war, US military personnel are estimated to have fathered 30,000 to 40,000 children with Vietnamese women.[9] Most abandoned their families when they left Vietnam, and many mothers also rejected their child because of a social taboo against these Amerasian children, who were referred to as the "dust of life". Many were left in under-equipped orphanages where food was scarce. Some were taken to the United States or other countries for adoption during Operation Babylift, when US forces airlifted around 4,000 children out of Saigon at the end of the war.[10]

## The Civil War in Vietnam

**March 1973**
The last US troops leave Vietnam.

**August 1973**
The United States stops bombing Cambodia.

**January 1974**
Thieu declares that war has started again.

**August 1974**
In the United States, President Nixon resigns.

**March 1975**
The communists capture the South Vietnamese cities of Hue and Da Nang.

**21 April 1975**
Thieu resigns the presidency of South Vietnam.

**30 April 1975**
Communist forces capture Saigon.

# SURVIVING RE-EDUCATION

In the 1940s, Tran Ngoc Chau fought with the Viet Minh against the French. He then switched sides and joined them. He enlisted in the ARVN in 1954 and rose to become a lieutenant colonel. In 1966 Chau entered politics. By 1969 he predicted that the communists could not be beaten militarily and advocated negotiations. Angered by this, President Thieu had Chau arrested and sent to prison. When the communists took over the country in 1975, they also perceived him as a danger. Chau was sent to a re-education camp. He later described it:

*Our barracks had nothing but iron sheets for roofs, corrugated sheets for walls, and bare cement for floors. The compound was surrounded by high rows of concertina wire [large coils of barbed wire]. It was in the middle of this barren and deserted land.*[11]

▽ Prisoners peer out of a prisoner-of-war camp in Vietnam in 1973.

## A COMMUNIST EDUCATION

Many anti-communists were imprisoned at the camp, including former senior judges, members of the government, and police officers. After three tiring months of building the camp, they spent six months listening to lectures to "detoxicate" them from their Western ideas and impart Vietnamese communist principles.

Chau found the lectures interesting; although from a privileged background, he felt great compassion for poor people and remembered the comradeship he had experienced with the Viet Minh. The prisoners then returned to manual labour in the fields for twelve hours daily. It was so exhausting and stressful that some prisoners broke down and committed suicide.

## UNUSUAL PUNISHMENT

At the end of 1977, Chau was moved to Thu Duc prison in Saigon, reserved for dangerous criminals. Expecting to be shot dead, Chau was instead told to write his biography. The communists wanted to understand the viewpoint of anti-communists who opposed them because of their beliefs, in contrast to those who had simply been in the pay of the United States and motivated by self-interest.

After working for 58 days and submitting his 800-page biography, Chau was released, on the condition that he would serve his country. He was told to join the Social Sciences Institute and carry out a study of former South Vietnamese leaders. However, Chau was unwilling to inform on his friends so he and his wife secretly plotted to leave Vietnam.

Having learned Chinese while in prison under Thieu, Chau managed to smuggle his family out with a group of ethnic Chinese leaving Vietnam. For several months, they lived on a remote Indonesian island. One night, he heard an old US journalist friend of his, Keyes Beech, speaking on the radio. The Indonesians had sent a squad of police officers to guard them; he bribed one of them to send a telegram to Beech and ask for help. Chau had little hope that this would work. Yet to his astonishment, one month later, a helicopter arrived to rescue Chau and his family and take them to the United States.[12]

# THE AFTERMATH OF CONFLICT

Vietnam was devastated by the war and, in the following years, endured economic problems and further conflict with Cambodia. In the United States, questions were asked about why the superpower had failed to achieve its goals and whether it should ever have intervened in Vietnam. For those directly involved, the physical and psychological wounds lasted for decades.

## DEATH, DESTRUCTION, AND ECONOMIC RUIN

The war resulted in an enormous loss of life: around 2 million Vietnamese civilians and some 1.1 million North Vietnamese and NLF fighters died, while up to 250,000 ARVN soldiers perished. Many victims of napalm were grossly disfigured, and the incidence of cancer soared owing to the use of Agent Orange. At least 58,000 US soldiers lost their lives or went missing in action.[1]

Vietnam's industry, infrastructure, and resources had been ruined. During the war, China had provided rice to North Vietnam and the United States had supported the South. Now this assistance was withdrawn. In the immediate aftermath of war, many countries gave aid to Vietnam for reconstruction. The Soviet Union, for example, gave $3 billion.[2] However, the United States cut off all trade and aid. International banks, the International Monetary Fund, and the World Bank followed suit. There was virtually no Western investment in Vietnam until the 1990s.

## THE COLLECTIVIZATION DISASTER

Government policies made the economic difficulties worse. In 1977 the state began to **collectivize** agriculture in the south and in 1978 banned all private trade. The outcome was disastrous. The ethnic Chinese had once dominated the southern economy. Deprived of their business, they and many other middle-class Vietnamese fled the country by sea – they became known as the boat people. Vietnam lost around 1 million people who could have contributed to rebuilding the economy.[3] By 1979 it was clear that collectivization was a failure, too. Many peasants refused to work hard on the collective farms because they preferred to work their own land. Grain shortages occurred, and the government had to introduce food rationing.

In 1986 the government adopted the Doi Moi economic policy. It allowed peasants to sell goods in the market economy and welcomed foreign investment to build its industry and services. It achieved economic growth and dramatically reduced poverty. However, inequality increased.

## The killing fields of Cambodia

The 1970 US invasion of Cambodia (see page 34) led to divisions between the Cambodian government, which supported the US intervention, and the communist opposition. Many people supported the Khmer Rouge, a Chinese-backed communist party, because it opposed the US attacks on Cambodia.

Led by Pol Pot, the Khmer Rouge seized power in Cambodia in 1975 and attempted to push through a rapid peasant revolution. Millions of people were evacuated from the cities and forced to become unpaid workers in farming collectives or labour camps. Money, private ownership of property, education, and religion were abolished in this radical revolution. Pol Pot told his supporters to "smash" the enemy – the upper, middle, and educated classes – and they slaughtered around 1.5 million people in massacres that became known as the "killing fields".

The revolution failed, and an estimated 20 per cent of the population died from starvation, overwork, disease, or execution.[4] In 1978 Vietnam invaded and installed a Vietnamese-backed government.

## PERCEPTIONS OF THE WAR

In Vietnam an official account of the war developed from the North Vietnamese communist perspective. According to this, the North had won an extraordinary victory owing to the heroic self-sacrifice of its people, united under siege. Around the country, war monuments were constructed to honour the dead. Etched on the top were words such as, "The Fatherland Remembers Your Sacrifice". The state offered medals to mothers who had lost at least three children in the war. However, there was no room in this account for the South Vietnamese, and no government support for the families of those who had died fighting for South Vietnam.

Although it was quite common to have family members fighting on both sides, their relatives were shamed into concealing the history of those who died for the South. On the family altar, they displayed only the photographs of those who died for communism. However, by the 1990s many families decided it was time to honour all the victims. People were no longer ashamed to have relatives who fought on the South Vietnamese side.

▷ This relative of a soldier who died in the war is visiting the Vietnam War Memorial in Washington DC in 1988.

## A RANGE OF VIEWS

As soon as the war was over, a debate arose within the US military and academic establishments: how was the most powerful country in the world defeated by a small, poor nation? Former Secretary of State Dean Rusk believed the United States should have used maximum force right from the outset: "President Kennedy should have put in a hundred thousand troops immediately."[5] From the other side, former PAVN general Van Tien Dung thought that the United States failed because the GIs were unsuccessful at guerrilla warfare.

The political aspects of the war were discussed, too. The use of huge military force had not persuaded the resistance to surrender but had the opposite effect, pushing more people into the arms of the NLF. Some critics argued that the excessive use of violence in Vietnam was not only unsuccessful but also immoral. Professor Richard Falk stated that it was a "violation of the international standards of law which the US itself had established".[6]

In the United States, postwar views were shaped by Hollywood films. Many, such as *Apocalypse Now* (1979), depicted the horror and deep psychological impact of the conflict. However, the Hollywood viewpoint was narrow, portraying small units of courageous US infantrymen combating an almost invisible enemy. The Vietnamese were rarely shown. Nevertheless, a survey in 1982 indicated that more than 70 per cent of the public believed the war was "fundamentally wrong and immoral".[7]

### Fighting for freedom?

President Ronald Reagan, speaking at Veterans Day in 1988, adopted the Hollywood view of patriotic US troops fighting for freedom. However, this was an uncommon view of the war in 1988:

*"And yet after more than a decade of desperate boat people, after the killing fields of Cambodia, after all that has happened in that unhappy part of the world, who can doubt that the cause for which our men fought was just?"[8]*

## VETERANS' VOICES

US veterans expressed mixed feelings about the conflict. A 1980 study of US veterans indicated that they remained patriotic; 71 per cent said that they were glad to have gone to Vietnam.[9] Yet, they had become increasingly disillusioned as the war progressed. Many blamed the political leadership for the defeat – 82 per cent complained that they had been sent to fight a war that "the political leaders in Washington would not let them win".[10] When many veterans returned, they felt that society did not appreciate their sacrifice because they had lost the war. Dave Christian explained, "I came back with hundreds and hundreds of crippled [disabled] men whose bodies were wrecked in Vietnam and we aren't perceived with dignity."[11]

△ Ron Kovic (centre) was a prominent member of VVAW. Here, he is leading a protest held in 2008 against the second US-led war in Iraq.

For a lot of soldiers, the war never completely ended. For decades after the war, they bore the physical effects of injuries or chemical warfare, or suffered psychological problems. One survey in 1988 showed that, of the three million soldiers who had served in Vietnam, half a million experienced **post-traumatic stress disorder**.[12] More veterans than the average experienced divorce, drug addiction, and particularly alcoholism, while some were so depressed they committed suicide.

## LEARNING THE LESSONS

The United States ended the draft in 1973, relying instead on volunteer soldiers, and did not initiate full-scale military intervention in another country until the First Gulf War of 1991. Then it organized a military coalition with several other countries to share the task of attacking Iraq, which had invaded Kuwait. The military establishment tightly controlled media coverage to prevent the spread of negative stories about its actions.

However, echoes of Vietnam are apparent in the Afghanistan and Iraq conflicts. The United States utilized overwhelming military power to invade and occupy these countries in 2001 and 2003 respectively. Similar to the Vietnamization policy in South Vietnam, it has attempted to replace US troops with local forces in Iraq and Afghanistan. As of 2011, the US military has remained involved in both countries. Has US policy in Iraq and Afghanistan been any more successful than it was in Vietnam?

### Could war have been avoided?

After the war, former Secretary of Defence Robert McNamara believed there were "misunderstandings" between the United States and Vietnam that could have been resolved to avert the conflict. In the mid-1990s, he held a personal meeting with North Vietnamese military leader Vo Nguyen Giap to discuss the issue. Vo Nguyen Giap disputed McNamara's interpretation, replying, "I don't believe we misunderstood you. You were the enemy; you wished to defeat us – to destroy us. So we were forced to fight you – to fight a 'people's war' to reclaim our country from your neoimperialist [modern-day imperialist] ally in Saigon."[13]

# BAO NINH: *THE SORROW OF WAR*

Bao Ninh is a North Vietnamese veteran of the war. In 1991 he published his novel *The Sorrow of War*, written from the perspective of a 17-year-old boy who volunteers for the PAVN. Ninh was the first Vietnamese author to dare to describe the brutality of the war and the damage it inflicted on the survivors and their loved ones. Initially banned by the Vietnamese government, it soon became a bestseller, especially loved by former soldiers, both Vietnamese and American.

## KIEN'S LIFE

The book weaves between the main character Kien's wartime experiences and his later life in Hanoi. It documents Kien's transformation from a keen young recruit to a sad, lonely veteran who is very critical of the military leadership and angry at the lack of respect shown in the post-war period to those who sacrificed their youth and health for the war effort.

▽ These NLF guerrillas are advancing under covering fire from a heavy machine gun in 1968.

## HORROR AND HEROISM

Bao Ninh's novel shows how some ordinary people acted with great brutality amid the violent circumstances of war. When Kien first travels south to join his battalion, his girlfriend Phuong recklessly decides to go with him. Their train is bombed by US soldiers. When Kien seeks out Phuong in the wreckage of the carriage afterwards, he finds her being violently attacked. She survives but is greatly disturbed. "It was from that moment, when Phuong was violently taken from him that the bloodshed truly began and his life entered into bloody suffering and failure."[14]

The conflict also brought out true heroism. Kien remembers a teenage scout called Hoa who became lost while trying to lead a group of wounded men out of danger. While trying to find their route, he and Hoa spot a group of US soldiers with a tracker dog. They know the soldiers will soon find the injured fighters. Hoa shoots the dog but the US soldiers chase and catch her; she is viciously attacked and killed. Hoa's actions have saved Kien, who then leads the wounded to safety.

In 1976 Kien returns with the Missing in Action body-collecting team to the Central Highlands, where his battalion was wiped out in 1969. The area is known as the "Jungle of Screaming Souls" because so many died there. For Buddhists, it is important to recover the bodies of "lost souls" who otherwise cannot rest. However for Kien, there is no rest; the sorrows of war will remain with him forever.

## Death is normal

Bao Ninh shows clearly how normal forms of behaviour are often discarded in times of war, and how people become used to death. On 30 April, the day the North Vietnamese take Saigon, Kien is the only survivor of a scout platoon sent to the airport. Exhausted, he falls asleep only to wake up to find he has been sleeping next to the naked corpse of a young woman. "I was so tired I didn't notice her," he says.[15]

# WHAT HAVE WE LEARNED?

Owing to the Cold War, the United States became involved in Vietnam when the war with France ended in 1954. North Vietnam, North Korea, and China had become communist, and US leaders believed it was crucial to support South Vietnam to prevent the other countries in the region falling to communism. It was determined to prevail in South-East Asia.

## WHY DID THE UNITED STATES FAIL IN SOUTH VIETNAM?

The US-backed South Vietnamese government relied on a narrow base of support and suffered from poor leadership and corruption. Meanwhile, the NLF had policies that much of the population thought were fairer, and wanted to achieve a unified independent Vietnam. They therefore grew increasingly popular and committed to the struggle. After the United States pulled out of South Vietnam in 1973, the Saigon government was too weak to survive.

## THE MEDIA AND THE ANTI-WAR MOVEMENT

The United States did not restrict reporters as much as they later would. For the first time, viewers saw the gruesome reality of war on television. Anti-war sentiments surged after significant events, such as the Tet Offensive and the My Lai massacre, were exposed in the media. From 1968, the anti-war movement grew in strength and put pressure on Nixon's administration. However, the importance of the protests in forcing Nixon to withdraw US troops is a matter of debate.

## HOW WAS THE UNITED STATES DEFEATED?

The resistance movement in Vietnam played the biggest role in the US defeat. The United States believed it could bomb Vietnam into submission. Yet the more bombs the US forces dropped, the more people joined the resistance and became determined to fight for an independent nation.

## THE LEGACY OF THE WAR

The conflict left Vietnam impoverished with a weak economy; the communists found it harder to rule successfully in peacetime than during the war. Cambodia was plunged into further crisis. Meanwhile, the United States did not initiate direct military intervention against another country until 1991. In the early 21st century, however, it led the invasion and occupation of Afghanistan and Iraq. Was the United States no longer restrained by the memory of Vietnam?

## THE BEST OF BOTH WORLDS

Thirty years after the war with the United States ended, North Vietnamese writer Huu Ngoc believed that although the Vietnamese hated the Americans during the war, this was no longer the case. Ngoc saw benefits of both cultures: "I think the strength of Vietnamese culture is that we stress the spiritual side of life and live for other people. But that's also our weakness. If you are too collectivist-minded you can't develop your individuality. In America ... people are governed by individualism. So we have to marry the best of both cultures."[1]

# TIMELINE

| | |
|---|---|
| **1887** | France creates the Indo-Chinese Union, which includes Vietnam, Cambodia, and, from 1893, Laos |
| **1930** | Ho Chi Minh founds the Indo-Chinese Communist Party |
| **May 1941** | Vietnamese communists set up the Independence League of Vietnam (Viet Minh) |
| **9 March 1945** | Japan takes over the French administration throughout Indo-China |
| **July 1945** | At the Potsdam Conference, Britain is assigned to take control in South Vietnam while the Chinese are to reassert control in the North |
| **2 September 1945** | Ho Chi Minh declares independence in North Vietnam |
| **23 November 1946** | French forces bombard Haiphong |
| **1 October 1949** | Mao Zedong proclaims the establishment of the People's Republic of China |
| **January 1950** | The Soviet Union and China recognize North Vietnam |
| **26 June 1950** | North Korea invades South Korea |
| **7 May 1954** | The Viet Minh defeats the French at Dien Bien Phu |
| **July 1954** | Under the Geneva agreement, Vietnam is divided into the Democratic Republic of Vietnam in the North and the Republic of Vietnam in the South |
| **23 October 1955** | Ngo Dinh Diem wins elections and declares himself head of South Vietnam three days later |
| **May 1959** | North Vietnam starts smuggling fighters and equipment to South Vietnam using the Ho Chi Minh Trail |
| **April 1960** | North Vietnam brings in universal military conscription |
| **20 December 1960** | The National Liberation Front for South Vietnam (NLF) is formed |
| **June 1963** | A Buddhist monk commits suicide in an anti-government protest, and Buddhist protests increase |
| **1 November 1963** | Diem is ousted in a military coup |
| **22 November 1963** | US President John F. Kennedy is assassinated and replaced by Lyndon Johnson |
| **2 August 1964** | North Vietnamese patrol boats attack a US destroyer in the Gulf of Tonkin |
| **7 February 1965** | NLF military forces attack US installations in South Vietnam; Johnson immediately orders Operation Flaming Dart, an aerial bombing campaign against North Vietnam |

| | |
|---|---|
| 24 February 1965 | Operation Rolling Thunder, the sustained US bombing of North Vietnam, begins |
| 8 March 1965 | The first US combat troops arrive in South Vietnam |
| March 1965 | The anti-war movement begins in the United States |
| October 1965 | US forces defeat three North Vietnamese regiments in the Ia Drang valley |
| 1966 | The Fulbright Hearings are held to debate the war |
| 3 September 1967 | Nguyen van Thieu becomes president of South Vietnam |
| 31 January 1968 | The Tet Offensive begins |
| 16 March 1968 | The My Lai massacre takes place |
| May 1968 | Peace talks take place in Paris, France |
| 5 November 1968 | Richard Nixon wins the US presidential election |
| 18 March 1969 | Nixon begins the secret bombing of Cambodia |
| 8 June 1969 | Nixon begins withdrawing US troops from Vietnam |
| August 1969 | National Security Adviser Henry Kissinger holds the first secret meetings with North Vietnamese negotiator Xuan Thuy in Paris; Le Duc Tho soon takes over from Xuan Thuy |
| November 1969 | Lieutenant Calley is court-martialled for ordering the My Lai massacre |
| 29 April 1970 | Nixon launches attacks by US and South Vietnamese forces on communist bases in Cambodia |
| 4 May 1970 | Four students are shot dead at a protest at Kent State University, Ohio |
| 30 June 1970 | Nixon withdraws US troops from Cambodia |
| February 1971 | South Vietnamese troops invade Laos |
| March 1972 | North Vietnam launches an attack on South Vietnam |
| 18 December 1972 | Nixon orders the bombing of Hanoi and Haiphong |
| 23 January 1973 | A ceasefire is agreed at the Paris Peace Conference |
| 9 August 1974 | Nixon is forced to resign |
| 17 April 1975 | The Khmer Rouge takes power in Cambodia |
| 21 April 1975 | Thieu resigns as president of South Vietnam |
| 30 April 1975 | Communist forces capture Saigon |
| 2 July 1976 | The Socialist Republic of Vietnam is proclaimed |
| 1977 | The Vietnamese government collectivizes agriculture in the south |
| 1978 | All private trade is banned |
| November 1978 | Thousands of ethnic Chinese people begin to flee Vietnam |
| 25 December 1978 | Vietnam invades Cambodia |
| 1986 | The Vietnamese government brings in the Doi Moi economic policy |
| 1995 | The United States resumes diplomatic relations with Vietnam |

# GLOSSARY

**ally** countries, people, or organizations that co-operate with each other

**Amerasian** in Vietnam, a child with a US father and a Vietnamese mother

**artillery** large, heavy guns, which are often moved on wheels

**assassinate** murder; usually the killing of a well-known person for political reasons

**barbarism** cruel or violent behaviour

**battalion** large body of troops

**black nationalist** person who belonged to the US movement in the 1960s and 1970s that sought to achieve economic power and build a sense of community feeling among African Americans

**ceasefire** when enemies agree to stop fighting

**censorship** when a state or organization controls information and may prevent it from being published or broadcast

**civilian** person not in the armed forces

**coalition** union of different political parties that come together to rule or a group of nations that work together to achieve a particular aim

**collectivize** when the government takes over the ownership of the land and groups of people farm it together

**colonize** when one country controls and rules another

**colony** country that is ruled by another country

**communist** political system where the government owns and controls industry, such as farms, mines, and factories

**Congress** in the United States, the group of people who are elected to make laws. Congress consists of the Senate and the House of Representatives.

**conscription** ordering people by law to serve in the armed forces

**conventional** in Vietnam warfare, battles between armies rather than guerrilla warfare

**corrupt** willing to do dishonest things in return for money

**coup** sudden, illegal, and often violent change of government

**covert** secret

**desertion** when a person leaves the armed forces without permission

**discriminate** treat a particular group in society unfairly, for example because of their race or sex

**draft** compulsory recruitment to the army

**exile** someone who has had to go to live in another country, particularly for political reasons

**exploit** make use of and gain benefit from someone or something, often unfairly

**feudal** social system in which landowners held land that peasants lived and worked on in return for protection by the landowners

**GI** ordinary soldier in the US armed forces, literally, a "government issue"

**grenade** small bomb that can be thrown by hand or fired from a gun

**guerrilla** fighter against a regular army

**imperialism** policy whereby one country controls other countries through military force or economic means

**infantrymen** soldiers that fight on foot

**land reform** dividing farmland into smaller parts so that more people can own some land

**Marine** soldier who is trained to serve on land or at sea

**napalm** jelly-like substance, made from petrol, which was used in some bombs in Vietnam. It burns on contact with the body.

**National Guard** army of each state in the United States

**nationalist** someone who is committed to the independence of his or her country

**occupy** move troops into another country and take control of it using military force

**offensive** military operation in which soldiers launch an attack

**post-traumatic stress disorder** medical condition in which a person suffers from psychological and emotional problems because of a difficult experience in the past

**progressive** in favour of new ideas, modern methods, and change

**re-education camp** in Vietnam, prison camps set up after the Vietnam War to teach people considered to be enemies of the government to change their thinking

**repressive** controlling people by force and restricting their freedom

**revolution** when a group of people organize to change the government of a country

**rig** organize in a dishonest way to achieve a particular result

**self-immolation** burning oneself to death

**Senate** one of the two groups of elected people who make laws in the United States

**shrapnel** small pieces of metal that are thrown outwards from an exploding bomb

**Soviet Union** state made up of Russia and several neighbouring countries. The Soviet Union was in existence from 1922–1991.

**stalemate** situation in a dispute in which neither side can win or make any progress

**strafe** attack from a low-flying aircraft using bullets or bombs

**teach-in** informal lecture and discussion on a subject of public interest

**veteran** person who has been a soldier in a war

# NOTES ON SOURCES

**"Attack! Attack! Attack!" (pages 4–5)**
1. Christian G. Appy, *Vietnam: The Definitive Oral History* (London: Ebury Press, 2006), 302–3.
2. *Ibid*, 299–300.
3. Michael Hunt, (ed.) *A Vietnam War Reader* (London: Penguin Books, 2010), 157.

**War with France (pages 6–11)**
1. "Vietnam", Encyclopaedia Britannica, http://library.eb.co.uk/eb/article-52739. Accessed on 7 February 2011.
2. Mark Philip Bradley, *Vietnam at War* (Oxford: Oxford University Press, 2000), 34.
3. Jonathan Neale, *The American War in Vietnam 1960-1975* (London: Bookmarks Publications Ltd, 2001), 20.
4. *Ibid*, 19.
5. Mark Philip Bradley, *Vietnam at War*, 56.
6. "Ho Chi Minh", Encyclopaedia Britannica, http://library.eb.co.uk/eb/article-3229.
7. Lacouture, T., *Ho Chi Minh* (Harmondsworth: Penguin Books, 1967). Cited in Michael Gibson, *The War in Vietnam* (Hove: Wayland Publishers, 2001), 8.

**Enter the USA (pages 12–19)**
1. Mark Philip Bradley, *Vietnam at War*, 81.
2. Michael Maclear, *Vietnam: The Ten Thousand Day War* (London: Thames Mandarin, 1989), 79.
3. Mark Philip Bradley, *Vietnam at War*, 96.
4. *Ibid*.
5. Michael Hunt, (ed.) *A Vietnam War Reader*, 43. Punctuation added for clarity.
6. *Ibid*, 47.

7. Michael Gibson, *The War in Vietnam*, 33.
8. Connie Schultz, "The Vietnam War ended but a silent threat from Agent Orange remained: Unfinished Business", Cleveland.com, 30 January 2011, www.cleveland.com/agentorange/index.ssf/2011/01/the_vietnam_war_ended_but_a_si.html. Accessed on 7 February 2011.
9. Jonathan Neale, *The American War in Vietnam*, 70.
10. Mark Philip Bradley, *Vietnam at War*, 97.
11. *Ibid*, 101–2.
12. David Halberstam, *The Making of a Quagmire* (New York: Random House, 1965). Cited in Mark Philip Bradley, *Vietnam at War*, 77.
13. "Would JFK Have Left Vietnam?: An Exchange", *New York Review of Books*, 30 September 2010, www.nybooks.com/articles/archives/2010/sep/30/would-jfk-have-left-vietnam-exchange. Accessed on 7 February 2011.

**The US military goes in (pages 20–25)**
1. Christian G. Appy, *Vietnam: The Definitive Oral History*, 130.
2. Michael Maclear, *Vietnam: The Ten Thousand Day War*, 203.
3. Christian G. Appy, *Vietnam: The Definitive Oral History*, 17.
4. Stanley Karnow, *Vietnam A History: The First Complete Account of Vietnam at War* (Harmondsworth: Penguin Books, 1984), 467.
5. *Ibid*, 468.
6. *Ibid*, 472–3.

**Ongoing war (pages 26–35)**

1. Michael Gibson, *The War in Vietnam*, 20.
2. "Vietnam War, Tet brings the war home", Encyclopaedia Britannica, http://library.eb.co.uk/eb/article-234636?query=Tet%20offensive&ct=. Accessed on 7 February 2011.
3. Michael Hunt, (ed.) *A Vietnam War Reader*, 172.
4. Mark Philip Bradley, *Vietnam at War*, 154–5.
5. Jonathan Neale, *The American War in Vietnam*, 63.
6. *Ibid*.
7. *Ibid*, 62.
8. *Ibid*, 65–6.
9. "Bomb Live Unit (BLU-82B)", National Museum of the US Air Force, www.nationalmuseum.af.mil/factsheets/factsheet.asp?id=1013. Accessed on 7 February 2011.
10. Michael Maclear, *Vietnam: The Ten Thousand Day War*, 212.
11. "AH-1 Cobra", Global Security.org, www.globalsecurity.org/military/systems/aircraft/ah-1-specs.htm. Accessed on 7 February 2011.
12. Dwayne A. Day, "Helicopters at War", U.S. Centennial of Flight Commission, www.centennialofflight.gov/essay/Rotary/Heli_at_War/HE14.htm. Accessed on 7 February 2011.
13. Michael Herr, *Dispatches* (London: Picador, 1978). Cited in Michael Gibson, *The War in Vietnam*, 29.
14. Mark Philip Bradley, *Vietnam at War*, 159.
15. Michael Maclear, *Vietnam: The Ten Thousand Day War*, 402.
16. Mark Philip Bradley, *Vietnam at War*, 160.
17. Michael Maclear, *Vietnam: The Ten Thousand Day War*, 422.
18. *Ibid*, 413–4.

**Living through the war (pages 36–43)**

1. Mark Philip Bradley, *Vietnam at War*, 118.
2. *Ibid*.
3. *Ibid*, 121.
4. Michael Hunt, (ed.) *A Vietnam War Reader*, 152–3.
5. Spencer Tucker, *Vietnam* (Kentucky: University Press of Kentucky, 1999), 120.
6. Mark Philip Bradley, *Vietnam at War*, 129.
7. *Ibid*, 130.
8. *Ibid*, 131.
9. Michael Gibson, *The War in Vietnam*, 36.
10. Michael Maclear, *Vietnam: The Ten Thousand Day War*, 328.
11. Jonathan Neale, *The American War in Vietnam*, 71.
12. Christian G. Appy, *Vietnam: The Definitive Oral History*, 157.
13. Stanley Karnow, *Vietnam A History*, 469.
14. Vivienne Sanders, *The USA and Vietnam 1945-75* (London: Hodder Murray, 2007), 121.
15. *Ibid*.
16. Stanley Karnow, *Vietnam A History*, 26.
17. Michael Maclear, *Vietnam: The Ten Thousand Day War*, 375–6.
18. Jonathan Neale, *The American War in Vietnam*, 102–3.
19. Michael Maclear, *Vietnam: The Ten Thousand Day War*, 378.

**The anti-war movement (pages 44–51)**

1. Michael Maclear, *Vietnam: The Ten Thousand Day War*, 309–10.
2. Jonathan Neale, *The American War in Vietnam*, 87.
3. Michael Maclear, *Vietnam: The Ten Thousand Day War*, 314.
4. *Ibid*, 318.
5. Christian G. Appy, *Vietnam: The Definitive Oral History*, 262.
6. Michael Hunt, (ed.) *A Vietnam War Reader*, 168–9.
7. Christian G. Appy, *Vietnam: The Definitive Oral History*, 238.
8. Michael Maclear, *Vietnam: The Ten Thousand Day War*, 301.
9. *Ibid*, 302.

10. George Plimpton, "Muhammad Ali: The Greatest", *Time*, 14 June 1999, www.time.com/time/magazine/article/0,9171,991256,00.html. Accessed on 7 February 2011.
11. Michael Maclear, *Vietnam: The Ten Thousand Day War*, 313.
12. *Ibid*, 313.
13. *Ibid*.
14. Jonathan Neale, *The American War in Vietnam*, 125.
15. *Ibid*, 123.
16. *Ibid*, 128.
17. Michael Maclear, *Vietnam: The Ten Thousand Day War*, 371.
18. *Ibid*, 372.
19. Jonathan Neale, *The American War in Vietnam*, 85.
20. Michael Maclear, *Vietnam: The Ten Thousand Day War*, 309–10.
21. Jonathan Neale, *The American War in Vietnam*, 87.
22. Michael Maclear, *Vietnam: The Ten Thousand Day War*, 395.
23. Jonathan Neale, *The American War in Vietnam*, 111.
24. *Ibid*, 112.
25. Michael Maclear, *Vietnam: The Ten Thousand Day War*, 404.
26. Vivienne Sanders, *The USA and Vietnam 1945-75*, 171.

**Vietnam united (pages 52–57)**
1. Cited in Mark Philip Bradley, *Vietnam at War*, 170.
2. Stanley Karnow, *Vietnam A History*, 660–61.
3. Mark Philip Bradley, *Vietnam at War*, 170.
4. Michael Hunt, (ed.) *A Vietnam War Reader*, 190.
5. Nixon To Thieu, 5 January 1973, in Nguyen Tien Hung and Jerrold L. Schecter, *The Palace File* (New York: Harper & Row, 1986), 392. Cited in *Ibid*, 171.
6. Stanley Karnow, *Vietnam A History*, 669.
7. Michael Hunt, (ed.) *A Vietnam War Reader*, 196.

8. "Amerasian Act", web.e.com/joelarkin/MontereyDemographicHistory/Amerasian_Act.html. Accessed on 7 February 2011.
9. "Amerasian Act". Accessed on 7 February 2011.
10. "Precious Cargo", PBS, www.pbs.org/itvs/preciouscargo/babylift.html. Accessed on 7 February 2011.
11. Christian G. Appy, *Vietnam: The Definitive Oral History*, 476.
12. *Ibid*, 475–80.

**The aftermath of conflict (pages 58–65)**
1. "Vietnam War", Encyclopaedia Britannica, http://library.eb.co.uk/eb/article-9075317?query=Vietnam%20war&ct=. Accessed on 7 February 2011.
2. Michael Maclear, *Vietnam: The Ten Thousand Day War*, 470.
3. Mark Philip Bradley, *Vietnam at War*, 176.
4. "Cambodia", Encyclopaedia Britannica, http://library.eb.co.uk/eb/article-52489. Accessed on 7 February 2011.
5. Michael Maclear, *Vietnam: The Ten Thousand Day War*, 475.
6. *Ibid*, 477.
7. Michael Gibson, *The War in Vietnam*, 51.
8. Michael Hunt, (ed.) *A Vietnam War Reader*, 202.
9. Stanley Karnow, *Vietnam A History*, 466.
10. *Ibid*.
11. Michael Maclear, *Vietnam: The Ten Thousand Day War*, 382.
12. Vivienne Sanders, *The USA and Vietnam 1945-75*, 190.
13. Michael Hunt, (ed.) *A Vietnam War Reader*, 203-4.
14. Bao Ninh, *The Sorrow of War* (London: Minerva, 1994), 167.
15. *Ibid*, 93.

**What have we learned? (pages 66–67)**
1. Christian G. Appy, *Vietnam: The Definitive Oral History*, 546-7.

# BIBLIOGRAPHY

Appy, Christian G. *Vietnam: The Definitive Oral History*, Ebury Press, 2006.

Bao Ninh. *The Sorrow of War*, Minerva, 1994.

Bradley, Mark Philip. *Vietnam at War*, Oxford University Press, 2000.

Gibson, Michael. *The War in Vietnam*, Wayland Publishers, 2001.

Hunt, Michael (ed.). *A Vietnam War Reader*, Penguin Books, 2010.

Karnow, Stanley. *Vietnam A History: The First Complete Account of Vietnam at War*, Penguin Books, 1984.

Maclear, Michael. *Vietnam: The Ten Thousand Day War*, Thames Mandarin, 1989.

Neale, Jonathan. *The American War in Vietnam 1960-1975*, Bookmarks Publications Ltd, 2001.

Sanders, Vivienne. *The USA and Vietnam 1945-75*, Hodder Murray, 2007.

# FIND OUT MORE

## BOOKS
### Non-fiction
Daugherty, Leo J. *Vietnam War. Facts At Your Fingertips: Military History,* Wayland, 2011.

Daynes, Katie. *The Vietnam War*, Usborne, 2008.

Kent, Deborah. *The Vietnam War: From Da Nang to Saigon (United States at War)*, Enslow Publishers, 2011.

Perritano, John. *Vietnam War (America at War)*, Scholastic, 2010.

Sanders, Vivienne. *The USA and Vietnam 1945–75*, Hodder Murray, 2007.

Watts, Anne. *Always the Children: A Nurse's Story of Home and War*, Simon and Schuster, 2010.

Yarborough, Trin. *Surviving Twice: Amerasian Children of the Vietnam War*, Potomac Books, 2006.

### Fiction
Bao Ninh. *The Sorrow of War*, Vintage Books, 2005.

Choyce, Lesley. *Reckless*, Orca Book Publishers, 2010.

O'Roark Dowell, Frances. *Shooting the Moon*, Turtleback Books, 2009.

Partridge, Elizabeth. *Dogtag Summer*, Bloomsbury Children's Books, 2011.

## DOCUMENTARIES
*The Vietnam War with Walter Cronkite*, Quantum Leap, 2007.

## WEBSITES
http://memory.loc.gov/frd/cs/vntoc.html
Find out more about Vietnam on the Library of Congress site.

www.pbs.org/wgbh/amex/vietnam/
The US broadcasting company PBS site details the US experience of the war but also includes essays by Vietnamese people.

www.spartacus.schoolnet.co.uk/vietweb.htm
This page has many links to sites including the history of the war, women's roles, veterans' experiences, and Vietnam Veterans Against the War.

# FURTHER TOPICS FOR RESEARCH

Large numbers of US soldiers were captured during the Vietnam War and endured great hardship. There are stories of US Prisoners of War on the Library of Congress website.

If you have enjoyed reading the personal stories in this book, investigate some oral history materials. For US oral history, start with the links on the Library of Congress site. You can find the stories of women who served in Vietnam, too. You may also like to investigate the particular experiences of black soldiers.

Soldiers from Australia, New Zealand, and South Korea also fought in Vietnam; you could research their experiences.

You may want to find out more about Vietnamese perspectives on the war. There is a growing body of resources available in English.

# INDEX

Afghanistan conflict 63
African Americans
  civil rights movement
    45, 48
  GIs 40, 45, 48
Agent Orange 16–17
Ali, Muhammad 46–47
Amerasian children 55
anti-personnel cluster bombs
  30
anti-war movement 25, 27,
    41, 44–51, 66
  civil rights movement
    45, 48
  draft resistance 44, 45,
    46–47
  Fulbright hearings 45
  GIs 48–49
  protest songs 37
  students 44, 50–51
  veterans 25, 48, 49
Army of the Republic of
  Vietnam (ARNV) 12, 13,
    21, 28–29, 34, 36, 51
atrocities 41, 42–43, 61

B-52 bombing raids 30
Bao Dai 8, 13
Bao Ninh 64–65
boat people 58
body bags 46
bombing campaigns 21, 28,
    30, 35, 38, 66
  Cambodia 30, 34, 53
  Laos 30
  napalm 5, 30, 46, 58
  North Vietnam 21, 28, 30,
    35, 38
  South Vietnam 30
Buddhist demonstrations
    18–19

Calley, Lieutenant William L.
    42, 43
Cambodia 6, 12, 14, 35, 67
  bombing of 30, 34, 53
  invasion of 28, 34, 50, 59
  Khmer Rouge 59
camouflage 39
casualties
  American 23, 27, 58

civilian 17, 18, 22, 34,
    38, 58
  North Vietnamese 27, 58
  South Vietnamese 27, 58
censorship 38, 46
Central Office for Southern
  Vietnam (COSVN) 34
chemical warfare 15, 16–17
China 8, 10, 21, 58
Chinook helicopters 32, 40
"Christmas bombings" 35
civil rights movement 45, 48
civilians
casualties 17, 18, 22, 34, 38
  evacuation 39
  impact of war on 36–37
  peasantry 12, 15, 16,
    36, 59
  refugees 36
Cold War 8, 66
collectivization 58–59
colonialism 6, 7, 8, 11
combat refusal 48
communism 6, 7, 8, 10,
    11, 12, 14, 15, 20,
    40, 55, 66
conscription 12
conventional warfare 22
cordon-and-search missions
    24–25
Cronkite, Walter 27
Cuba 14

daisy cutter bombs 31
Democratic Republic of
  Vietnam (DRV) see North
  Vietnam
desertion 47
Diem Bien Phu, battle of 8,
    9, 18, 19
Doi Moi economic policy 59
domino theory 14
draft 22, 40
  end of 63
  resistance 44, 45, 46–47
drug use 37, 41

Easter Offensive 35
Ehrhart, William 24–25, 41
environmental degradation
    16–17, 39

famine 7
"fragging" incidents 49
France
defeated at Dien Bien Phu 9
French Indo-China 6, 7, 8, 11
free-fire zones 36
Fulbright, J. William 45

Geneva Agreement 8
GIs 40–41, 45
combat refusal 48
  deserters 47
  "fragging" incidents 49
  morale 41
  see also veterans
guerrilla warfare 11, 13, 15,
    16, 21, 22–23, 61
Gulf of Tonkin incident 20
Gulf War 63

Hanoi 7, 8, 35, 54
helicopters 32–33, 40
  gunships 30, 32
  transport helicopters 32,
    32–33
Ho Chi Minh 6, 7, 8, 9,
    10–11
Ho Chi Minh Trail 12, 16,
    21, 34
Hue 5, 27

Ia Drang Valley, battle of
    22, 33
Indo-China 6, 7, 8, 11
Iraq 63

Japan 7
Johnson, Lyndon 20, 21,
    22, 27
journalism 46, 48

Kennedy, John F 14, 15,
    19, 61
Kent State University protest
    50–51
Khmer Rouge 59
King, Martin Luther 45, 49
Kissinger, Henry 29, 34, 35
Korean War 8

land reforms 9, 11, 14, 15
Laos 6, 12, 14, 35
  bombing of 30
  invasion of 28, 34
Le Duan 54
Le Duc Tho 35

McNamara, Robert 15, 63
madman theory 34, 35
media coverage 27, 46, 63, 66
MiG planes 31
military technology 30–31
morale
  American troops 41
  North Vietnamese 38
My Lai massacre 42–43, 66

napalm 5, 30, 46, 58
National Liberation Front
  (NLF) 12, 13, 15, 18, 20,
    21, 24, 26, 27, 29, 34,
    36, 41, 53, 61, 66
nationalism 7, 11
  black 48
Ngo Dinh Diem 8, 12, 13
Nguyen Chi Thanh, General
  21
Nguyen Ngoc, General 4
Nguyen Van Thieu 52, 53, 56
Nixon, Richard 28, 29, 34,
    35, 49, 50, 51, 53, 66
North Vietnam 6, 7, 8, 11
  armies 4, 12, 21, 22, 33,
    36, 39, 53
  bombing of 21, 28, 30,
    35, 38
  Chinese/Soviet aid 8, 21,
    30, 31, 58
  impact of war on 38–39
  military technology 31
  proclaimed as Democratic
    Republic of Vietnam
    (DRV) 7

Operation Babylift 55
Operation Flaming Dart 21
Operation Phoenix 29
Operation Ranch Hand
  16–17
Operation Rolling Thunder
  21, 38

patriotism 61, 62
People's Army of Vietnam
  (PAVN) 4, 21, 22, 33,
    39, 53

People's Liberation Armed
  Forces (PLAF) 12, 21,
    36, 53
Pol Pot 59
post-traumatic stress disorder
  62
prostitution 37, 41

radar systems 31
re-education camps 54,
  56–57
Reagan, Ronald 61
remote-control detection 30
Rusk, Dean 15, 61
Russian Revolution 10, 14

Saigon 12, 27, 57
  capture of 53–54
search and destroy missions
  22, 23
self-immolations 18–19
The Sorrow of War 64–65
South Vietnam 6, 8, 9, 20
  army 12, 13, 21, 28–29,
    34, 36, 51
  bombing of 30
  defeat of 53–55
  impact of the war on
    36–37
  impact of Western culture
    on 37
  peasantry 12, 15, 36
  poor leadership and
    corruption 36, 52, 66
  US economic and military
    support 8, 9, 12, 15, 29,
    36, 52
Soviet Union 8, 10, 21, 58
surface-to-air missiles
  (SAMs) 31, 33

Tet Offensive 4–5, 25, 26–27,
  46, 66
Thich Quang Duc 18
total war 38
Tran Ngoc Chau 56–57
tunnel networks 23

United States
  anti-communism 9, 14, 15,
    20, 40, 66
  anti-war movement 25, 27,
    41, 44–51, 66
  civil rights movement
    45, 48
  draft 22, 40

  economic and military
    support for South Vietnam
    8, 9, 12, 15, 29, 36, 52
  impact of war on 61–63
  military technology 30
  policies towards Vietnam
    15, 19
  reasons for defeat of 66, 67
  sends troops to Vietnam
    20, 22
  strategy 28–29, 30, 34–35
  troop numbers 22, 23
  withdrawal from Vietnam
    51
USS Maddox 20

Van Tien Dung, General 61
veterans 17, 62, 64
  anti-war movement 25,
    48, 49
  physical and psychological
    problems 62
Viet Cong see National
  Liberation Front (NLF)
Viet Minh 7, 9, 11
Vietnam
  colonial era 6, 7
  division 8
  impact of war on 36–39,
    58–69, 67
  reunification 54, 55
Vietnam Veterans Against the
  War (VVAW) 25, 49, 62
Vietnam War
  ceasefire 35, 52
  cinematic portrayal of 61
  media coverage of 38,
    46, 66
  origins of conflict 6–20
  peace talks 27, 28, 35
  postwar impact of 58–59
  US withdrawal 51
Vietnam War Memorial 60
Vietnamization policy
  28–29, 34
Vo Nguyen Giap 63

war crimes 41, 42–43
war memorials 60
Watergate 28, 53
Westmoreland, General 22,
  23, 27, 32, 33
women
  combat forces 22, 23,
    36, 39
war work 39